Introduction

This book provides an opportunity for children to discover interesting and unusual facts about our planet and the people on it. They will learn about plants and living creatures; how men and women have made astonishing conquests; how they have built incredible structures and machines.

There are four main sections – ANIMALS, THE NATURAL WORLD, PEOPLE and the MAN-MADE WORLD. These are subdivided to cover: *on the land* – from plains to mountains and from police around the world to famous buildings; *in the water* – from hot springs to the ocean depths; and *in the air* – from the sky to outer space.

The section on ANIMALS includes a large variety of species, grouped to focus attention on characteristics, unusual behaviour, similarities and differences. The NATURAL WORLD section deals with plants and strange wonders beneath, on and above the Earth's surface. Included in the section on PEOPLE are contrasting customs, environments and backgrounds. The MAN-MADE section deals with modern technology, ranging from computers to trains, from oil rigs to aircraft. All countries mentioned are shown on double-page maps of the world. This helps readers to build up an overall picture with a constant reference.

This book will excite children's natural curiosity and imagination. It will stimulate interest in acquiring further knowledge about the world around them. More than 400 superb pictures bring the book to life. The text is designed for young readers. OUR AMAZING WORLD covers an interest level for children from 5 to 10 years.

ISBN 0 86112 364 6
© BRIMAX BOOKS LTD 1986. All rights reserved
Published by Brimax Books, Newmarket, England 1986
Printed in Hungary

OUR
AMAZING
WORLD

Editor
Stephen Attmore

Artists
Graham Allen
Bob Bampton
John Blackman and
  Mandy Doyle
Tony Gibbons
Terry Hadler
Bob Hersey
Eric Kincaid
Alan Male
Colin Newman
Jack Pelling
John Rignall
David Thompson
Brian Watson

Cover design by Sebastian Quigley
Cover illustration by Bob Bampton

Acknowledgements

Survival Anglia: (A. Root) 17, (J. & D. Bartlett) 25TR, (J. Foott) 52L, 56TL; **Eric and David Hosking**: 20, 21C; **Frank Lane Picture Agency**: 21B, 45T, 48, 59L; **OSF**: (B. Watts) 25TL, (P. Parks) 31TL, 38CL, (M. Fogden) 45B, (K. Sandved) 53T, (G. I. Bernard) 65L; **NHPA**: (A. Bannister) 25BL/BR; **ARDEA LONDON**: (P. Morris) 30, 31TR/C/L; (J. Mason) 57, 129BL, (L. & T. Bamford) 56TR, (J. Ferrero) 62TL/TR, (A. Warren) 65TL, (F. Gohier) 65TR, (R. Bunge) 130BL; **Heather Angel**: 38CR, 53C; **Bruce Coleman**: (J. Burton) 40, (J. & D. Bartlett) 52R, (C. Hughes) 56B; **Natural Science Photos**: (C. Mattison) 41; **ZEFA**: 59R, 62LR, 63TL, 67BL, 67B, 68B, 95TR, 121TL/BL, 129R, 131B; **Camerapix Hutchison Library**: 60L, 68T; **Japan Tourist Organisation**: 60R, 120; **Picturepoint – LONDON**: 60T, 67BL, 113BR; **Colorific**: (T. Carr) 62BL, (D. Hunt) 113BL; **Mike Andrews**: 63TR, 130BL, 142B; **The Photo Source**: 63B; **Robin Smith Photography**: 67TL; **Brian and Cherry Alexander**: 69L; **BAS**: (C. K. Gilbert) 68R; **Fred Bruemmer**: 71; **NASA**: 76, 77, 78, 79T, 109BL, 133T; **The Daily Telegraph**: 79C; **Susan Griggs Agency**: 91C, 95TL, 121R, 128BL/BR, 129TL, 130TL/TC/TR, 131T, 133L; **VISION INTERNATIONAL**: (M. Mann) 91T, (G. Blond) 98L, (A. Driver) 99C, (P. Koch) 132; **Popperfoto**: 98R; **Sporting Pictures (UK) Ltd**: 99B; **Shell Photograph**: 104; **Novosti Press Agency**: 109TL/TR; **The RAF Falcons**: 112; **RAF**: 113T; **Associated Press**: 115; **London Express News and Feature Services**: 117; **Science Photo Library**: (J. Walsh) 122T, (W. M. McIntyre) 122BR; **Heffers Printers Ltd**: 122BL; **'Flight International'**: 123, 144TL, 148; **Sonia Halliday**: 128TL; **Barnaby's Picture Library**: 128TR; **Planet Earth Pictures/SEAPHOT**: 136; **U S Treasury**: 142T, 144BL; **British Tourist Authority**: 144TR; **The J. Allan Cash Photolibrary**: 144BR; 61T is reproduced by permission of Director, British Geological Survey (NERC) – NERC copyright reserved; 67TR courtesy of New Zealand Tourist Office; © **Crown**: 146; 149 – reproduced with kind permission of the Controller of Her Majesty's Stationery Office; 14TR/L – used by kind permission of Tesco Training Services

OUR
AMAZING
WORLD

FASCINATING
FACTS

Karen O'Callaghan

BRIMAX BOOKS · NEWMARKET · ENGLAND

Contents

ANIMALS AND THE NATURAL WORLD

PEOPLE AND THE MAN-MADE WORLD

ANIMALS
and the
NATURAL WORLD

ANIMALS
On the land

The **African bull** (male) **elephant** is the largest animal on land. It can weigh 6 tonnes and it eats up to half a tonne of plant food every day.

A **giraffe** is the tallest animal. It sleeps standing up, and cannot make any sounds or calls. The tallest giraffe was 5·8 metres (20 feet).

The longest snake is the **reticulated python** from South-East Asia. It can be 9 metres (29·5 feet) long. It is not poisonous but kills by squeezing its victim.

The **komodo dragon** is the largest lizard. It lives only on the island of Komodo in Indonesia and can be nearly 3 metres (10 feet) long.

The **Galapagos giant tortoise** is the largest land tortoise. It can weigh 226 kilos (500 lbs) and can live to be 152 years old.

The **cheetah** is the fastest animal on land. It can reach speeds of 112 kilometres per hour (70 miles per hour), over short distances.

How baby animals travel

Some babies are carried in a special pouch on their mother's stomach.

koala

kangaroo

After 5 or 6 months in the pouch, the baby koala climbs on to its mother's back.

The **Virginia opossum** has many babies. They are so tiny when they are born that 13 little babies would fit on a teaspoon. When they become too big for the pouch they climb on to her back and cling on to her fur with their toes and tails.

giant anteater

pangolin

Both the **giant anteater** and the **pangolin** carry their babies on their backs, near their tails. When danger threatens, the mother pangolin cuddles her baby inside her curled-up body. She uses her scales to protect them.

14

A **shrew** usually has six babies. When they leave their nest they must stay together for safety. The mother shrew leads the way. Each baby holds the tail of the one in front, in its mouth. They all move off together in a line.

baboon

sloth

These babies cling to the underside of their mother's fur.

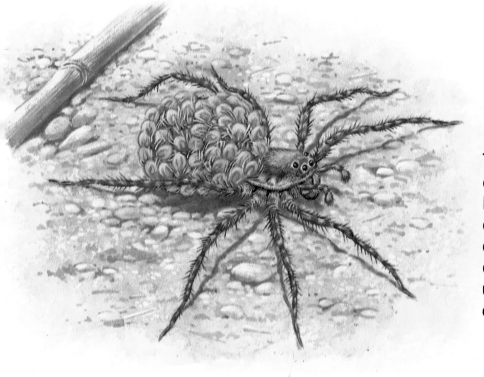

The **wolf spider** drags her egg-sack behind her as she hunts for food. Once the eggs hatch, the babies cluster on her back. She carries them like this until they are one week old.

Defence tricks

Many animals use special tricks to defend themselves against attack by their enemies.

The **opossum** will hiss at an attacker to try to scare it. If this does not work, it falls down and pretends to be dead. It stays still and the enemy may leave it alone.

The **hognose snake** rolls on its back with its mouth wide open, not moving. If it is turned over it will flip on to its back again. The enemy thinks it is dead.

hedgehog

porcupine

Both the **hedgehog** and the **porcupine** have sharp quills, like needles. When they roll into a ball they become very difficult to attack.

A **frilled lizard** hopes to scare its attacker. It gulps in air. Its body puffs up, making it look bigger. Also a frill pops out just below its mouth.

A **skunk** raises its tail and sprays its enemy. The spray stings and has a very bad smell.

If attacked, a **cuscus** chatters loudly and gives off a horrible smell.

The **chuckwalla** is one of the largest lizards in the USA. When attacked, it will crawl into a space between two rocks. It will then puff itself up with air so that it cannot be pulled out. If it is caught by its tail, the tail breaks off and the chuckwalla escapes. A new tail grows within a few weeks.

17

Hunter attackers

Driver ants from Africa march in columns five or six across.
They form a closely-packed group of thousands of ants.
If something blocks their way, they will make a chain or bridge
to get across. They eat cockroaches, snakes, cattle, gorillas or
any injured animal.

Lions are not fast runners, so they
rely on team-work. They hunt as
a group. It is usually the females
(lionesses) that do the hunting.

lioness stalking

prey

lioness waiting

A group of lionesses hunting.

Special tricks

This **web-throwing spider** comes from South Africa. At night it weaves a web, about the size of a stamp. It holds this between its long legs – and sits and waits. When a fly comes along, the spider stretches its web to six times the first size. The spider throws the web over the fly. Then the fly is helpless.

The **silk-throwing spider** comes from Australia. It spins a silken thread and places a drop of glue on the end. Then it lies in wait. As an insect approaches, the spider whirls the sticky thread round and round and throws it like a lasso.

The **ant-lion** is a trapper. It digs a small pit in dry or sandy soil. The pit is shaped like a funnel. The ant-lion buries itself at the bottom and waits. An insect, coming to the edge of the pit, finds itself slipping down the slippery sides. It is caught at the bottom.

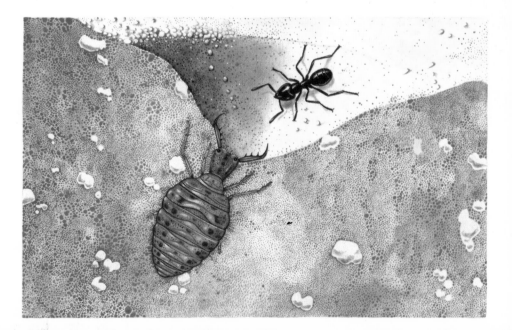

Animals with poison

Many animals attack and paralyse their victims with poison. The poison is called **venom**. It is usually injected by biting or stinging.

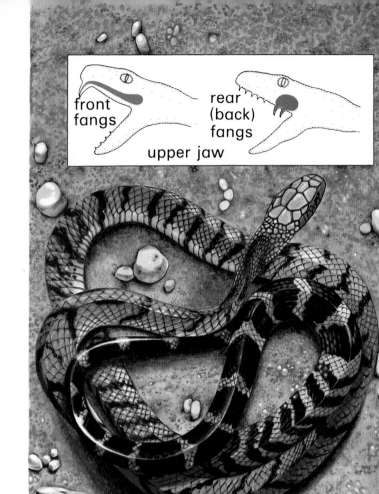

front fangs

rear (back) fangs

upper jaw

The **king cobra** is the largest poisonous snake. It lives in dense forests in Asia, near water. The king cobra feeds on other snakes and lizards. The cobra has fangs at the front of its upper jaw.

Snakes that kill by squeezing have solid teeth. Poisonous snakes have grooves down two teeth in the upper jaw. These are their fangs.

The most dangerous of the rear-fanged snakes is the African **boomslang**. These snakes bite their prey and then follow their victim. They follow its scent (smell), waiting for it to die from the poison. The snake smells with its tongue. Its forked tongue darts in and out, smelling the air.

The **gila monster** and the **Mexican beaded lizard** are the only types of lizard which are poisonous.

The **black widow spider** is the most dangerous spider. The male is small – 4 mm (¼ inch) – and harmless. The female is bigger – 13 mm (½ inch). Her venom is very powerful. The male keeps away from her most of the time, as she may eat him if she is hungry. The female has a shiny, black body with red markings underneath.

Scorpions have a sting at the end of their tail. If they attack a large animal, they hold it firmly with their pincers. Then they swing their tail over their head, giving their victim a quick stab of the sting. This paralyses the victim. Then it is eaten.

The **arrow poison frog** lives in South America. Its skin is sticky with poison. South American Indians dip their arrow heads in the poison. They shoot the arrows into small animals and the poison paralyses them.

Camouflage

Many animals have coloured bodies. Often their colouring protects them from their enemies because it makes them difficult to see. We call this **camouflage**. Animals use colours to hide, to change their shape, or to frighten and trick their enemies.

The **chameleon** can change the colour of its whole body very quickly. It will look green on the leaves and brown on the tree bark. When it is excited, the colours get brighter. When it is angry, the colours darken. When it is frightened, the colours get paler.

A **polar bear** is white all over except for its black nose. This helps it to hide in the snow. They have been known to cover their nose with snow when hunting seals.

A **gecko** has lots of spots over its body. This helps to break up the shape of the animal. When it stays still it is hard to see.

This North American **Io-silk moth** is on tree bark. It is very hard to find. If attacked, its back wings flick out flashing a pair of eyes.

The **praying mantis** looks like a leaf. It clings on to a leaf or stem. It is keeping very still, ready to strike.

The **dune wolf spider** is hiding amongst the stones and sand.

Do you know the difference?

A **crocodile** has a long, pointed face. When its mouth is closed the 4th tooth in its lower jaw pokes out.

An **alligator** has a broader face. Its 4th tooth fits into a groove in its upper jaw and does not stick out.

Monkeys like this **spider monkey** have tails. They use their tails like another arm, to swing or hold on to branches.

Apes have no tails. This gorilla is an ape. Others in the ape family are chimpanzees, gibbons and the orang-utan.

A **centipede** has about 30 legs. Some species (kinds) have more; others have fewer legs. They have one pair of legs under each section of their body.

A **millipede** has over 60 legs. They have two pairs of legs under each section of their body.

Beetles feed on greenfly and other bugs. These ladybirds are eating greenfly. Ladybirds are also called ladybugs.

Bugs suck sap (juices) from plants. Their mouth is like a hollow tube with a sharp tip. They suck up the sap like a syringe. Look at these **red-banded thrips**.

In the water

Do you know the difference?

Whales have soft smooth skin, and solid fins. They are mammals and give birth to live young. They have lungs and breathe through an air-hole on the top of their heads.

Fish have scaly skin and spiny fins. Most of them lay eggs. They breathe through gills.

gills

Seals have no ears.

Sea lions have ear flaps.

Turtles live in the water. **Tortoises** live on land.

A **frog** has smooth skin, long legs and moves in jumps.

A **toad** has rough skin, shorter legs and usually it runs.

The **blue whale** is the biggest animal in the world. It is the largest animal of all time. It weighs more than 30 elephants and can be 30 m (98 feet) long.

The **sperm whale** can dive deeper than any other whale. It can go down to nearly 1000 m (3281 ft). It can stay under the water for up to one hour.

Sailfish are the fastest swimmers. They can reach speeds of 90 km/h (56 mph), over short distances.

The **walrus** is the only animal that walks on its teeth. It uses its tusks as a weapon. It also uses them to pull itself out of the sea and to pull itself along on the land.

Special ways of attack

The **archer fish** can catch insects that are on plants out of the water. It uses its tongue like a water gun. It fires a water bullet at the insect, knocking it off the leaf and into the water.

Piranha fish are fierce hunters. They live in the large rivers of South America and hunt in groups. They have mouths filled with razor-sharp teeth. Piranhas are the animal world's greatest eaters. They take bites out of animals of any size.

The **deep-sea angler fish** lives in the Atlantic Ocean. It is usually found 3½ miles down below the surface of the sea where there is no light. It has a fishing pole attached above its mouth. This shines like a light. When it waves the pole about, little fish think it is food. They come too close and are caught.

Poisonous creatures

Many creatures in the sea use poison. They use it either as an attack or as a defence, to prevent themselves from being eaten.

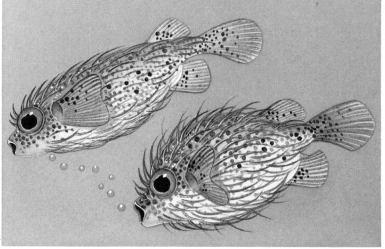

The **lionfish** has poisonous spines. It is also brightly coloured. This is a warning to other fish that it is dangerous.

The **porcupine fish** is another spiny creature. It takes in air, which blows up the body like a balloon. This makes the spines stand up and stick out.

jellyfish

Jellyfish and **sea anemones** have tiny sting cells in their tentacles (arms).

sea anemone

A **stingray** has a sharp spine on its tail which contains venom. When it is attacked, it whips its tail and the spine sticks into the victim's skin.

triggerfish   puffer fish

These fish have poison in their bodies. This makes them very dangerous to eat.

Cone snails live on coral reefs. They have a tooth on their nose that injects venom.

Sea urchins have sharp spines. Their venom is on the tips of the spines.

Helping each other

Remoras and **sharks** – remoras are sometimes called sucker fish. They have a suction pad on their heads. They hitch a ride on the body of a shark. They feed on the small animals that stick to the shark's skin.

Goby fish and **pistal prawns** live together in the same burrow. The prawn is the worker. It digs out the burrow and keeps it clear of sand. It shovels the sand with its pincers. The prawns are blind. The goby fish act as sentries at the opening of the burrow. They leave first and tap their tails to signal that it is safe for the prawns. The goby watches for sea snakes and other enemies.

Clown fish swim in and out of the tentacles of a **sea anemone**, but they do not get stung. They lay their eggs at the base of the tentacles. There they are safe from enemies. When other fish try to attack the clown fish, the sea anemone stings with its tentacles. Both animals eat the victim.

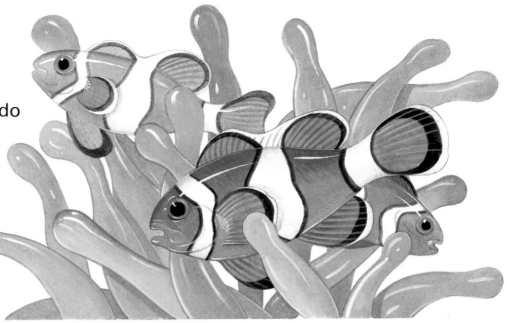

Cleaner wrasse are very small fish about 10 cm (3·9 inches) long. They live in warm tropical waters. Their food is dead skin from the body and gills of other fish. They also swim into the mouths of larger fish to take scraps of food stuck in between the teeth. They approach other fish with a wriggling motion. This seems to prevent them from being eaten.

Hermit crabs crawl around on the seabed, scratching in the sand for food. The **sea anemone** rides on the top of the crab's shell. The anemone catches scraps of food, as the crab is eating. The anemone's tentacles also help to protect the crab from attack.

Monsters of the deep

The surface of the sea is always moving, but deep down the water is still. Strange fish live in the deepest depths of the ocean – between 250 m (820 ft) to 4000 m (13,123 ft). It is always cold and dark. It is a dangerous place. As fish hunt for food, other fish hunt them. There are no plants growing, so the deep-sea fishes eat each other. As it is dark, the fish make their own light. Most of them have a strong sense of smell and good hearing.

The **gulper eel** can swallow a fish several times its own size. Its jaws open very wide and its skin stretches over its victim. It has a light on its tail.

The **oarfish** can be 9 m (29·5 feet) long. The fin all along its back gleams a bright red colour in the darkness.

The **black swallower** has a wide head and sharp teeth. It is long and thin – until it has eaten. Then its stomach stretches like a bag. It does not have to eat often.

The female **angler fish** lures small fish into her open mouth with a shining rod on her head. The female is 61 cm (2 feet) long and the male is only 10 cm (4 inches) long.

The **squid** squirts a cloud of liquid into the water to escape from an enemy.

Deep sea dragonfish have teeth which shine in the dark. They also have lights round the eyes and along their bodies.

Taking care of the babies

Many sea creatures lay their eggs and then leave them. When the baby sea creatures hatch out of their eggs, they have to find food for themselves. Other sea creatures take great care of their babies and protect them until they can take care of themselves.

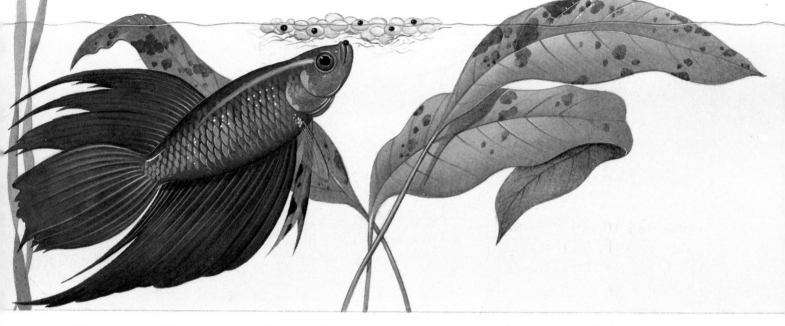

The male **Siamese fighting fish** builds a nest of bubbles. This floats on the top of the water. As the female lays her eggs, the male catches them one by one in his mouth. Then the male swims up to the bubbles on the surface. He sticks each egg on to the raft of bubbles. Then he swims round and round, watching them.

The male **sunfish** makes a shallow, round nest in the sand close to the shore. The female lays her eggs and then swims away. It is the male that stays to take care of the babies.

The female **seahorse** places her eggs inside a pouch on the male's stomach. The pouch has many compartments, one for each baby. The young will stay in the pouch until they are fully grown. Then the pouch will open and the babies swim free.

Sticklebacks make a nest of water weeds. If the tiny sticklebacks swim away from the nest, the male will chase them. He sucks them into his mouth and spits them back into the nest.

The female **sea catfish** places her eggs in the male's mouth. He carries them carefully in his mouth for about one month. When they hatch, they stay in the male's mouth until they have grown to about 5 cm (2 inches) long.

37

Special swimmers

An **octopus** has eight arms with rows of suckers on each of them. It walks along the seabed or swims by squirting out a jet of water which pushes it forwards.

The **seahorse** swims upright in the water. The fin on its back moves and drives it forwards.

Jellyfish cannot swim, but drift and are carried by the wind and water currents. This **Portuguese man-of-war** has a poisonous sting in its tentacle.

Ordinary fish breathe by taking in oxygen (air) from the water. They do this by opening and closing their mouths, pushing water over their gills. A **shark** has gills but cannot pump the water. It has to keep swimming to push the water over its gills. A shark never stops swimming, even when asleep.

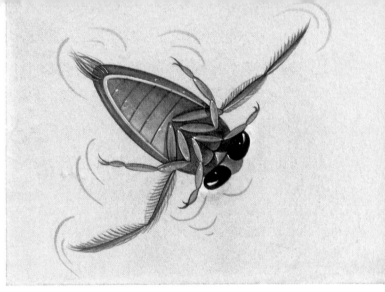

This **Goliath frog** from Africa is the largest of all frogs. Both frogs and toads hop or walk on land, but in water they swim breaststroke.

The **waterboatman** swims on its back on the surface of the water. It rows along with its back legs. It can also dive and swim under water.

Fish that can leave the water

Mudskippers live in tropical swamps. They leave the water to catch insects on land. To get out of water, a mudskipper curls its tail against the mud and jerks its body straight. These fish are only a few inches long.

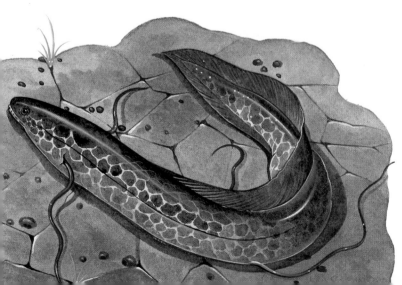

Lungfish can live in mud during the dry season in African swamps. As the pool dries up, the lungfish digs into the mud. It curls into a ball, wrapping its tail round its head. It breathes through small openings in its throat. These are simple lungs which breathe in air.

In the air

Flying animals

The **Atlantic four-wing flying fish** rises almost to the surface and swims at top speed rapidly vibrating its tail fin from side to side (50 beats per second). This acts as a propeller. The fish breaks the surface of the water and can fly up to 30 m (98 feet) at about 55 km/h (34 mph). It can also change direction as it is flying.

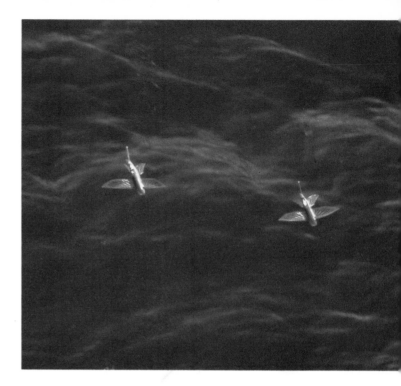

Flying squirrels have a membrane (skin) connecting their four paws. It runs along each side of the body, between the front and the hind legs. They jump off a branch and glide from tree to tree.

This **flying snake** from Asia lives in trees. When it launches itself from a tree top, it flattens its body, spreads its ribs and drives out all of the air from its lungs. It becomes very thin and flat. Then it can glide easily. It twists its body when it wants to change direction.

40

The **flying frog** of Borneo is the only type of frog that can fly. It has long toes, with wide webs between them. It spreads its feet to make flat gliding surfaces. It has sticky pads on its toes to help it hold on when landing.

The **flying gecko** stretches its webbed feet and flaps of skin at its side. This forms a parachute as it leaps into the air. It glides down.

The **flying dragon**, or **Draco**, of Borneo is a lizard. It has flaps of skin on each side of its body. When it rests these flaps are tucked into its body. Then it opens the flaps, throws itself into the air and glides to the next tree.

Birds that cannot fly

ostrich (Africa)

rhea (South America)

emu (Australia)

The **kiwi** lives in New Zealand. It spends its days in its burrow and comes out at night to search for food. It walks with the tip of its bill close to the ground sniffing for food. Unlike most birds, it has a very good sense of smell.

The **emperor penguin** lives in the Antarctic. Its wings have changed to fins, and its feet are webbed. It is an excellent swimmer and spends most of its life in water.

Snake hunters

The **roadrunner** lives in the dry deserts of America. It lives on the ground and only flies as a last resort – to escape danger. It always moves at a run, changing direction rapidly, so that it zigzags across the desert. As it runs, it holds its wings outstretched. The roadrunner is an expert snake catcher. It kills with its sharp beak. It is often seen running along with a snake hanging out of its mouth.

The **secretary bird** has a hooked beak and long talons. It flies and runs very fast. It walks faster than a human being can run. Secretary birds grow to 120 cm (4 feet). They sleep in trees at night and fly down in the morning to stalk through the grass. They strike and then jump back too quickly for any snake to attack them.

Flying attackers

Golden eagles soar high in the sky. Their eyesight is so good they can see the smallest movement, far below. The eagle drops from the sky at great speed to pounce on its victim. It dives at a speed of 160 km/h (100 mph).

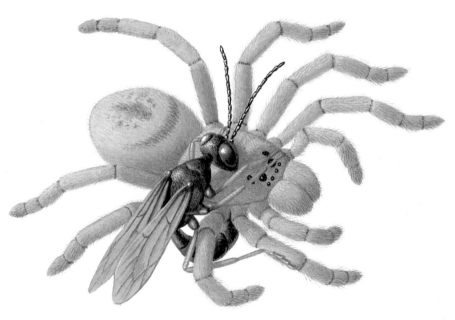

Tarantula hawk wasp – this wasp attacks tarantula spiders. It stings the spider and drags it, paralysed, into its hole. There it lays an egg on it. When the egg hatches out, the baby eats the spider.

The **Bengali fly** acts like a dive bomber. It hovers over **driver ants** on the march. The ants carry their young with them. The ant and the fly have a tug-of-war. When an ant puts down its young to fight, the fly snatches them and flies away.

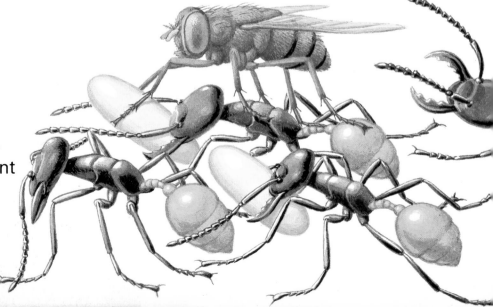

Homes

The **elf owl** (Mexico) is the smallest owl in the world. It is only 15 cm (6 inches) long. It lives in a hole in the saguaro cactus. It cannot peck out its own hole but uses an empty hole made by a woodpecker.

The **tailorbird** builds an unusual nest. With its sharp beak, it pierces holes along the edges of two leaves. It stitches the leaves together, using pieces of grass.

Weaver birds of Africa like to live together. As many as 150 weaver birds help to build the nest high up in a tree. Each pair of birds weaves a nest with grasses.

Flamingoes live together in large groups. They build their nests using mud, which they scoop up in their bills. The top of the nest is shaped like a cup so that the eggs do not roll out. Usually only one egg is laid and both parents take turns to sit on the nest.

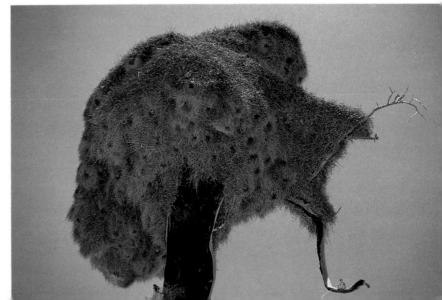

The **woodduck** makes her nest high up in a tree. In the spring when the chicks hatch, they jump out of the nest. They follow their mother duck and glide down to the ground.

A **kingfisher** digs its nest in the earth. It uses its long, pointed bill to dig out a tunnel in the river bank. At the end of the tunnel is a nesting chamber lined with fish bones.

The **sandgrouse** has her nest in the Kalahari Desert (Botswana, Africa). Each day the female leaves the young to fly many miles in search of water. She uses her breast feathers to soak up water. Then she flies back to the nest and the young birds suck the wet feathers for a drink.

When the female **great Indian hornbill** is ready to lay her eggs, she hides in a hole in a tree. The male seals up the hole. This leaves only a narrow slit through which the male passes food to the female who cannot get out. The eggs are safe from snakes and monkeys. The female stays with them until they are a few months old. Then she breaks out and helps the male to feed the chicks.

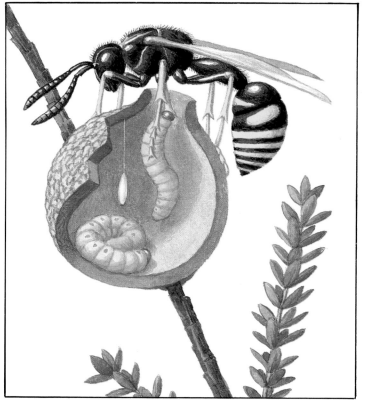

A **puffin** spends most of its time at sea. When it is ready to lay its eggs, it will build a nest on the cliffs. It digs a long tunnel, using its strong beak. It shovels out the earth with its webbed feet.

The **potter wasp** builds a nest of mud. The wasp puts caterpillars in the nest with the eggs. The caterpillars are food for the young when they hatch. Then the female wasp seals the top of the nest.

The **peregrine falcon** is the fastest moving animal. When in a dive, it swoops at 350 km/h (217½ mph).

The **ostrich** is the largest living bird. It lays the largest eggs. It can run very fast – 56 km/h (35 mph). The ostrich is the fastest animal on two legs.

The **hummingbird** is one of the smallest birds. It is so small, it would fit inside an egg cup. It can fly forwards and backwards. When it is feeding from a flower it hovers. Its wings beat at over 100 beats every second, making a humming noise.

The **Andean condor** has the largest wing area of any bird. It is often more than 3 m (10 ft) from tip to tip. This bird glides and soars high over the Andes in South America.

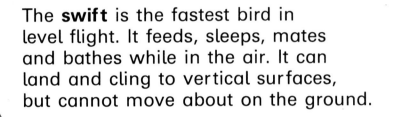

The **swift** is the fastest bird in level flight. It feeds, sleeps, mates and bathes while in the air. It can land and cling to vertical surfaces, but cannot move about on the ground.

The **Egyptian vulture** is one of the few birds that uses a tool. It picks up a stone and drops it on top of the egg. It does this again and again until the egg is cracked open.

49

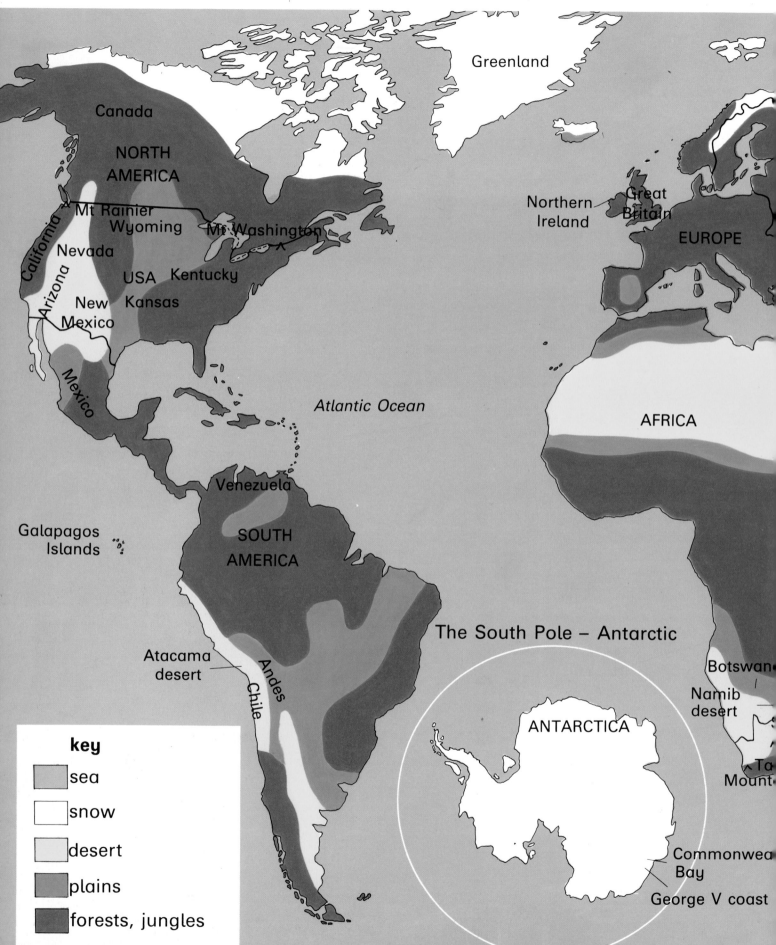

MAP OF

Greenland

Canada

NORTH
AMERICA

Mt Rainier
Wyoming
California
Nevada
Arizona
USA
New
Kansas
Mexico

Mt Washington

Kentucky

Mexico

Northern
Ireland

Great
Britain

EUROPE

Atlantic Ocean

AFRICA

Venezuela

Galapagos
Islands

SOUTH
AMERICA

The South Pole – Antarctic

Atacama
desert

Andes
Chile

Botswan

Namib
desert

ANTARCTICA

Ta
Mount

Commonwea
Bay

George V coast

key

- sea
- snow
- desert
- plains
- forests, jungles

THE WORLD

USSR (Russia)

Caspian
Sea

ASIA

Japan

Yellow
Sea

Jordan

Cherrapunji

China

West
Bengal

India

Hawaii

Pacific Ocean

Philippines

Marianas Trench

Borneo

Indonesia

Indian Ocean

Java

Komodo

The North Pole – Arctic

Kalahari
desert

ARCTIC

Arctic
Ocean

Australia

Greenland

New Zealand

51

THE NATURAL WORLD

On the land   Plants

The biggest tree in the world is the **Sequoia tree** in Sequoia National Park, California, USA. They grow up to 85 metres (279 feet) tall. They are up to 24 metres (78·7 feet) round. It is said that there would be enough wood to make 5000 million matches.

The largest **cactus** is the **saguaro**. It grows in American deserts to a height of 16 m (52 ft). American Indians use this plant for many things – the flesh and fruit for drinking, the seeds to make a kind of butter and the stem as a support for their tents.

The **rafflesia** is the largest flower in the world. It can be as wide as 90 cm (3 ft). It can weigh as much as 7 kg (15·4 lb). It grows in the forests of Indonesia.

The oldest trees in the world are the **bristlecone pines**. The oldest tree grows on a mountain in California. It is called 'Methuselah' and it is said to be 4600 years old.

The world's tallest trees are conifers. The **coast redwoods** of California, USA, grow to heights of over 75 metres. The tallest is 111·6 m (366 feet).

Giant waterlilies grow in South America. They have the largest leaves – 2 m (6½ feet) across.

Insect-eating plants

These plants cannot move to chase and catch their food. They use bait and a trap to catch small animals like flies, spiders, ants and other insects. The bait may be a bright colour, a special smell, or sweet nectar (juices). The trap is made by the leaves. It works in different ways in each plant.

The **Venus fly trap** is found in bogs and swamps in North America. The leaves form a hinged trap. When a fly lands on it the leaf snaps shut, trapping the fly inside. It takes half an hour for the fly to be squashed and killed. The trap stays shut for 5–10 days, while the fly is digested (eaten). Then the leaf opens and the skeleton (bones) is blown away by the wind.

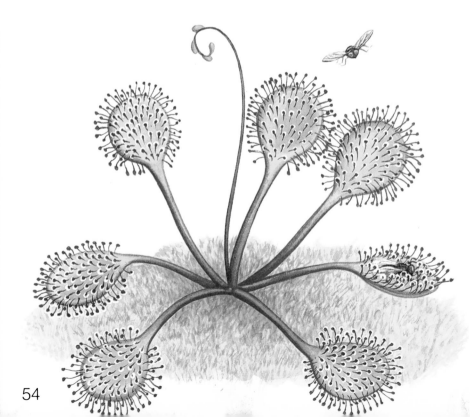

Sundews live in wet bogs, in South Africa. They trap insects with small, sticky tentacles on the leaf's surface. The tentacles have bright red heads, covered with sticky gum. As the fly lands on the leaf, it touches the tentacles. These bend over, trapping and holding the fly.

Pitcher plants grow in Australia. Parts of the leaves are shaped like jugs or pitchers. They have bright colours round the rim. The lid is half open, which stops rain getting in. The pitcher is half filled with liquid. When a fly lands on the edge, it slips down into the pitcher. The sides are too steep for it to climb out. It is trapped. Then it dissolves (melts) in the liquid.

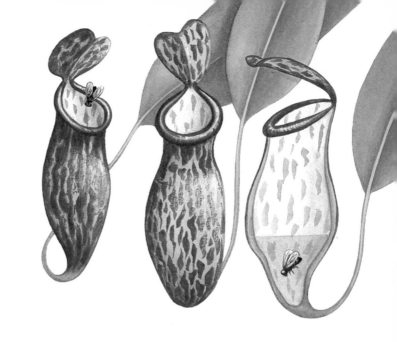

Butterworts grow in the northern parts of the world. The leaves are pale green, flat, shiny and sticky. They have an odd smell which attracts ants. The ant crawls on to the leaf and sticks to it. As it struggles, the leaf makes more sticky gum. The ant slowly dissolves and the plant takes in the food through the leaf.

Bladderworts are plants that grow in fresh water. They have many tiny sacs – like balloons – which are called bladders. They grow along a trailing stem. The bladders have a tiny opening in them, surrounded by bristles (hairs). Water fleas take shelter in the bristles. As they touch the bristles, the door shoots open. Then the door is sucked closed, trapping the flea.

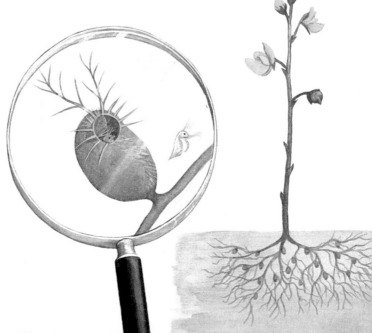

Unusual plants

The **Baobab tree** (right) grows in Africa. It stores water in its huge trunk, which can be 10 m (32·8 feet) wide. During the dry season, elephants often tear open the trunks to get at the soft watery insides.

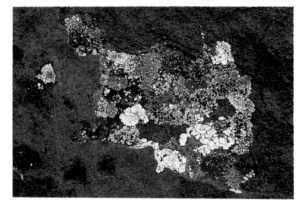

Lichens are tiny plants that grow on rocks. They make juices that eat into the rock and make it crumble. Their tiny roots eat the minerals in the rocks. The lichens slowly turn the rock into soil.

Stone plants grow in South Africa. Their leaves look like stones on the ground. This helps them to hide from animals that might eat them. The plants can only be seen when the flowers grow up between leaves.

Welwitschia mirabilis grows in the Namib desert, in Africa. It is more than 1000 years old. It takes the plant 20 years to grow its first flower. This plant has only two leaves. They split into thin strips.

All plants make seeds, for new plants to grow. They use many different ways to spread their seeds. Some use animals and insects to do this for them.

Fungi are a strange group of plants. They have no stems, roots or leaves. Many of them are poisonous. The **deathcap** is the most poisonous.

Cage fungi take only a few hours to grow. They make a black slime inside the cage that has a bad smell. Flies are attracted by the smell and eat the slime. They spread the spores to new places in their droppings.

Giant puffballs are fungi. This one measures 30 cm (11·8 in) across. It releases a cloud of its tiny spores (seeds) into the air. These are carried by the wind to new places. It makes 7 billion spores.

Mistletoe is sometimes called a vampire plant. It grows on trees and steals food and water from the tree. The mistletoe suckers force their way into the pipes that carry food and water round the tree.

The fruits of the **squirting cucumber** plant burst open, shooting the seeds out. The seeds travel at 100 km/h (62 mph). They can land as far away as 8 m (26¼ feet) from the plant.

The **coconut palm** grows close to the sea. The coconuts fall into the water. They are light and will float. The coconut is one of the few fruits that are spread by water.

The seeds from the **chinese lantern** plant are inside shiny red kites. They are carried by the wind.

Truffles are the fruits of a fungus. The plant uses animals to spread its seeds. A pig eats the fruits and the seeds inside pass through the pig's body unharmed. They are released again in the pig's droppings.

Volcanoes

The skin of the world, the part we live on, is called the Earth's crust. Deep down, many miles under the crust, it is so hot that the rock is soft. In some places it melts. When there is a crack in the crust, the melted (molten) rock is pushed up through the crack. The rock is then called **lava**. Sometimes it spills over, in streams of lava running down the sides of the volcano. Sometimes there are great explosions. The volcano erupts (spurts out) and the boiling lava is thrown high into the air.

Mount St Helens in America erupted throwing many tonnes of lava and rock high into the air. After the explosion the top of the mountain was 254 m (1000 feet) lower.

The volcanoes of Hawaii are like this. There is no explosion. The lava flows gently in rivers of fire down the mountain.

Many mountains around the world are volcanoes.

Kilimanjaro – East Africa

Mount Fuji-san – Japan

Lava builds up a cone-shaped mountain. There is a saucer-shaped hollow at the top, called a **crater**. When the lava cools down it becomes hard rock again. This is how volcanoes grow.

Around the world there are many very old volcanoes which died long ago. **Crater Lake** in North America was once a huge volcano. An explosion blew the top of the volcano off, leaving a hole (crater). It has now died and the crater has filled up with water, making a lake. It is 610 metres (2000 feet) deep and 9·6 km (6 miles) wide. There is a small island in the lake, called Wizard Island. This was a smaller volcano, which also died. When a volcano has died we say it is **extinct**.

Kilauea is in Hawaii. The name means 'rising smoke cloud'. Long ago its top fell in, leaving a deep, round crater. When Kilauea erupts, the lava is trapped in the crater. Visitors can stand on the edge and look down on the lake of boiling, bubbling lava.

Giant's Causeway is in Northern Ireland. Many years ago, molten rock was pushed up through the cracks and spilled over in rivers of lava. The lava cooled so quickly that it cracked into large columns. Most of these columns have six sides.

Amazing places

Ayers Rock in Australia is the largest block of stone in the world. It rises to a height of 279 m (1100 feet) and is 3·2 km (2 miles) long and 1·6 km (1 mile) wide. It is made of red sandstone.

Wave Rock is also in Australia. Over hundreds of years the wind, sand and weather have shaped the rock. It looks like a giant frozen wave.

Table Mountain is in South Africa. The top of the mountain is flat and is often covered by cloud or mist. People say this cloud is like a table cloth.

The **Chocolate Hills** are in the Philippines. Over 1000 hills are the same shape. During the winter, they are covered with grass. In the hot summer sun, the grass dries and turns a chocolate brown colour.

The largest cave system in the world is under the **Mammoth Cave National Park** in Kentucky, USA. There is a maze of caves and passages 307·5km (191 miles) long. Water drips from the roof and forms crystals. Those hanging down are **stalactites** and those rising up are **stalagmites**.

The **Painted Desert** is in Arizona, America. The hills are striped with colours. They are made from layers of different kinds of rock.

The **Colorado River** is in Arizona, America. It is the fastest navigable river. It rushes along at 32 km/h (30 mph), carrying small rocks and stones. Over hundreds of thousands of years these stones cut into the rock on either side of the river. This river has made the largest and deepest canyon in the world. In places the Grand Canyon is 1⅝ km (1 mile) deep and 24 km (15 miles) wide. It is about 321·8km (200 miles) long. Each year it is getting deeper and wider.

In the water

In 1883 **Krakatoa**, a famous volcano near Java, erupted with the biggest bang the world has ever known. A dust cloud formed 80·5 km (50 miles) up in the air. The island sank into the sea creating a huge wave 35 metres (115 feet) high.

before the explosion

after the explosion

The **Great Barrier Reef** is the largest coral reef in the world. It is off the north-east coast of Australia. It is 2500 km (1553 miles) long. The reef is built by tiny coral animals, which have feelers to catch food. Each animal builds itself a little stone cup to live in. The stone is left when the animal dies. New animals build more cups on top of the old ones. Very slowly the coral cups build up into a tall wall, called a **coral reef**. There are many different kinds and colours of corals.

The highest waterfall in the world is **Angel Falls** in Venezuela, South America. It is 979 m (3212 feet) high.

A **geyser** shoots a jet of boiling water and steam, high into the air. The highest is 457 m (1500 feet). One of the most famous is called 'Old Faithful' in Yellowstone National Park, Wyoming, USA. It gushes regularly once every hour.

Kelp is the fastest growing plant. It grows at a rate of 9 centimetres (3½ inches) every day. Many fish find food and shelter in the kelp forests.

Our watery world

Most of our world is water, which covers three-quarters of the Earth. There are five oceans – the Pacific (the largest), the Atlantic, the Arctic, the Antarctic and the Indian Ocean. There are also many seas. The floor of the sea is not flat. There are mountains, valleys and plains, just as there are on land.

There are deep valleys under the sea. The deepest are called **trenches**. If Mount Everest (the highest mountain) was dropped into the deepest trench it would not show above the surface of the water. The deepest trench is the **Marianas Trench** in the Pacific Ocean, south of Japan. It is 10,900 m deep (nearly 7 miles).

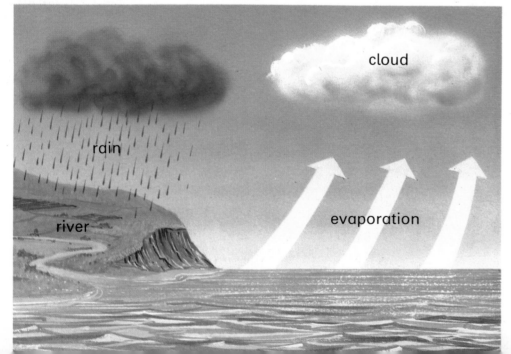

The water in the sea is salty. Rivers and streams flowing down from the land carry salty material down to the sea. The hot sun beating down on the sea's surface makes the water rise, like mist, into the air. The salt is left behind. This mist makes clouds and the water falls as rain over the land.

hot springs, Wairakei, New Zealand

mud pools, Rotorua, New Zealand

When it rains, some of the water seeps through the earth and small cracks in the rocks. This underground water may come out of the side of a mountain as a spring. When the water seeps down very deep to where the earth is hot, it is pushed up again and comes out as a **hot spring**. Sometimes the hot water makes pools of bubbling **hot mud**.

Caspian Sea

Lakes are made when water fills up hollows in the ground. The world's largest lake is in Russia – the **Caspian Sea**. It is so big it is called an inland sea. It is slightly salty.

The **Dead Sea** is also a salt lake. It is at the southern end of Jordan. It is the lowest point on the Earth's surface, 395 m (1296 ft) below sea level. The Dead Sea is so salty that swimmers do not sink and no fish can live there.

Rivers may start as springs high in the mountains. They flow down towards the sea. As the river pushes over rocks, small pieces break off and are carried along. The **Yellow River** in China carries yellow silt (pieces of rock smaller than sand). It stains the sea off the coast of China a yellow colour. It is called the **Yellow Sea**.

The **Niagara Falls** are on the border between Canada and America. It is not the highest waterfall, but it is the biggest. Hard rock forms a ledge right across the river. The water splashes over the hard rock and drops on to softer rock at the bottom. The force of the water carves away at the soft rock, forming a cliff.

Frozen water

In very cold countries and on high mountains, the rivers are ice instead of water. The ice is formed from the snow that falls on the mountains. The ice moves slowly down the slopes spreading outwards in **ice sheets** or **glaciers** (ice rivers). Where the edges of the ice sheets and glaciers reach the sea, huge blocks of ice break off. These are called **icebergs**. Ice is lighter than water so it floats. Some icebergs are as big as mountains.

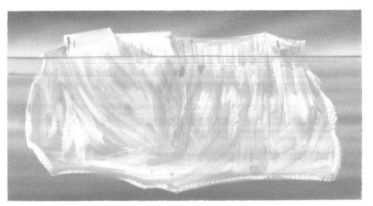

We see only the top (⅑ th) of the iceberg above the water.

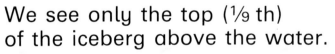
Great ice sheets cover Antarctica and Greenland.

The **icebergs** from **Antarctica** are mostly flat topped.

The **icebergs** from **Greenland** are high and jagged.

The ends of the world

The area round the **North Pole** is called the **Arctic**. It lies at the centre of the frozen Arctic Ocean. It is almost surrounded by land – Canada, Greenland, Europe and Russia. It is very, very cold, flat and open. In the summer, some of the ice sheet melts and the ice is carried round the pole in a clockwise direction. Greenland is a land of snow and ice. It is too cold for trees to grow. (85% of the land is covered with ice.)

The area around the **South Pole** is called the **Antarctic**. It is bigger than Europe and America put together. It is not on top of an ocean. It is land covered by ice and snow. The Antarctic is very cold and windy. (90% of the world's ice is in the Antarctic.) The ice can be up to 3500 m (11,483 feet) thick. It is mountainous. No plants grow on the ice and there are no land animals. Some scientists live in research stations, studying the weather. The Americans call their research station 'Deep Freeze'.

In the air

The midnight sun –
both the north and the
south poles have a time
when the sun never sets.
In the summer, there are
24 hours of daylight, and
in the winter there are
24 hours of darkness.
When the sun shines
at the North Pole the
South Pole is in darkness.

The **Northern lights** or
'Aurora Borealis' –
the auroras are caused by
light producing colours
and haloes in the sky.
These colours vary from
red to blue, and may last
for minutes or for several
days. It is like a curtain
of colour in the sky. The
southern aurora is called
the **'Aurora Australis'**.

atmosphere

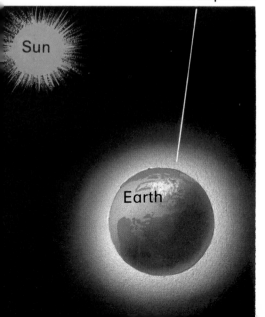

Around the Earth there is a great belt of air 200
miles high. It is called the **atmosphere**. The Sun
does not heat the atmosphere, it heats the ground.
Heat rises up from the ground. When air is warmed
it gets lighter and rises. The wind blows near
the surface, and high up in the air. When the wind
blows across the surface of the sea, rivers, lakes
and puddles, it carries some of the water into the
air as tiny invisible drops. This is how wet
clothes are dried by the wind. The rising damp
air meets cold air further up and forms clouds.

71

The weather

Clouds are made of millions of drops of water. The drops are so small and so light, they can stay up in the air. Tiny drops of water join together making big drops. These big drops are too heavy to float in the air. They fall to the ground as **rain**.

When the sun shines after a shower of rain we often see a **rainbow**. Light rays travel in a straight line, but they change direction when they pass through raindrops. Some colours bend more than others. They separate out to make a rainbow.

In clouds that are very high up, maybe 7 miles up, water droplets are pushed upwards. At the top, they collide with ice crystals. They trap air inside as they freeze, which makes them look white. They fall out of the clouds as **hailstones**.

When it is very cold, tiny drops of water in the clouds turn to ice. The ice crystals grow bigger and fall

as **snowflakes**. Each snowflake has a different pattern, but the shapes always have six sides.

Cherrapunji in north-east India holds the world record for the most **rain** – 9299 millimetres (36½ inches) in one month. The rains are so heavy they are called **monsoons**.

Hot deserts cover about one-fifth of the Earth's land. Some deserts get no rain. Parts of the **Atacama desert** in northern Chile have had no rain for 400 years.

The greatest **snowfall** ever recorded fell on Mt Rainier, Washington, USA. They found that 31 m (93 feet) of snow had fallen in one year.

The biggest **hailstone** ever measured fell in Kansas, USA, in 1970. It weighed 750 g (1·67 lb), was 19 cm (7½in) wide and 44·5 cm (17½in) round.

Storms

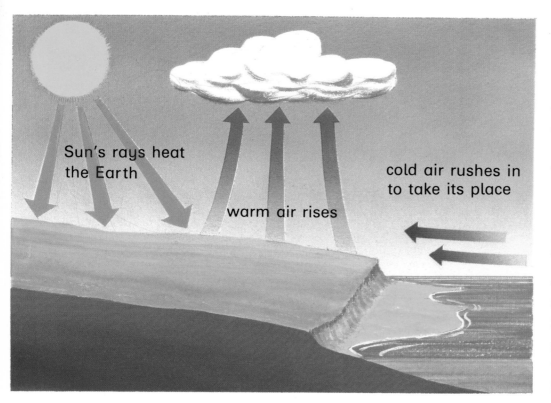

Sun's rays heat the Earth

warm air rises

cold air rushes in to take its place

Wind – when air is warmed it gets lighter and rises. Its pressure is then low. Cold air, which is heavier, has high pressure. The air moves from places where it is low. This moving air is the wind. Winds can be warm or cold, gentle or strong. The Beaufort Scale measures the strength of wind from Force 1 to Force 12.

Force 1 (2·5 km/h)
Smoke drifts; wind vanes do not move.

Force 2 (6–11 km/h)
Light breeze: leaves rustle; smoke drifts; flags flap.

Force 4 (20–29 km/h)
Moderate breeze: small branches move; flags fly.

Force 6 (40–50 km/h)
Strong breeze: large branches move; big waves.

Force 8 (62–74 km/h)
Fresh gale: walking hard; twigs break off trees.

Force 11 (103–120 km/h)
Storm: much widespread damage.

Lightning – when water droplets are being carried up and down in a thunder cloud, electricity is made at the top and bottom of the cloud. When electricity from one part meets electricity from another part it makes a spark. This is a lightning flash.

Thunder is the sound made by lightning. Air becomes hot along the flash. The heat moves the air so quickly that it makes a bang. The rumbling sound is the echo of the bang. Sound travels 1 mile in 5 seconds. If you count in seconds from the lightning flash to the first clap of thunder, then divide the number by 5, you will know how far away the storm is.

Tornado – sometimes when two kinds of air (hot and cold) try to pass each other they get locked together, and the air spins. During a tornado the winds spin round very fast making a funnel. This sucks things up like a vacuum cleaner. The funnel-shaped cloud twists and bends, and is sometimes called a 'twister'. It can cause a lot of damage.

A **waterspout** is a tornado that happens out at sea. The funnel of air sucks up a column of water. It usually lasts about half an hour.

A **hurricane** is a great storm that starts at sea, in hot weather. It is the worst kind of storm. These happen in many parts of the world and are given different names. In Australia they are called 'Willy-Willies', and in Asia cyclones or typhoons. The winds and clouds swirl round and round at speeds of 322 km/h (200 mph). At the centre there is no wind. It is called the 'eye' of the hurricane. Thousands of tonnes of rain form in the clouds. The winds are strong enough to blow down houses, uproot trees, lift cars and form giant waves.

The 'eye' of the hurricane seen from a satellite.

IT'S A RECORD

The greatest **wind speed** recorded was 371 km/h (231 mph) on Mt Washington, in New Hampshire, USA.

The **windiest place** in the world is Commonwealth Bay, George V coast in Antarctica. Gales and high winds here reach speeds of 320 km/h (200 mph)

In Space

day-time   night-time

During the daytime we can see blue sky and sunlight. We cannot
see Space. The sun shines so brightly, it is like a curtain of
light that we cannot see through. On a clear night, when the sun
has gone down, we can see stars and the Moon. The blackness all
around is Space.

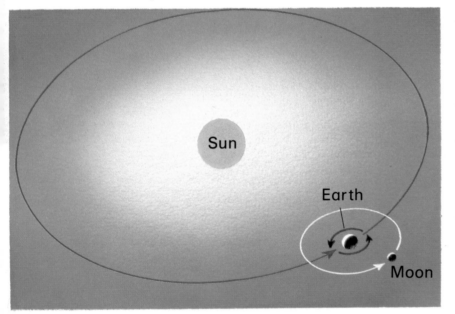

Our world, the **Earth**, is a planet.
It is a big ball (sphere) and it
travels in a huge circle
(orbit) around the Sun.
It takes one year for the
Earth to orbit round the
Sun.

The Earth is spinning all
the time. It takes a day
and a night to turn round
once.

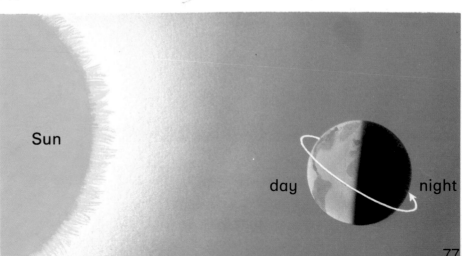

The **Sun** is very important to us, for heat and light. Without the Sun life on Earth would not be possible. The Sun is a sphere in Space. It is much bigger than the Earth. One million earths would fit into the Sun. It looks so small because it is so far away. It is 150 million km (93 million miles) away from us. It is a star, not a planet.

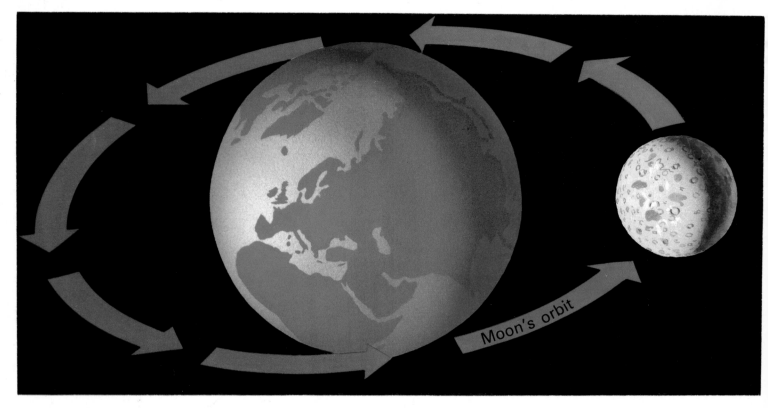

Moon's orbit

The **Moon** is also a sphere, spinning in Space. It is smaller than the Earth. It looks big because it is nearer to us. The Moon spins like a top round the Earth. Its journey takes four weeks.

We can see the Moon because the Sun shines on it. It reflects the light, like a huge mirror. It has light and dark patches on its surfaces. The light parts are mountains and the dark patches are flat plains and craters. The **craters** are huge holes, some as big as a city.

The Moon has no air, no water and no life on it. Sometimes we see just a part of the Moon, lit up by the Sun.

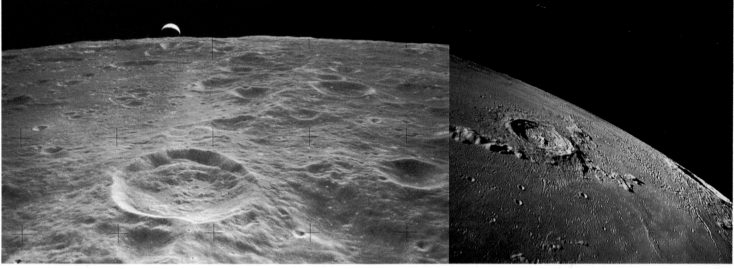

How many of these moon shapes have you seen?

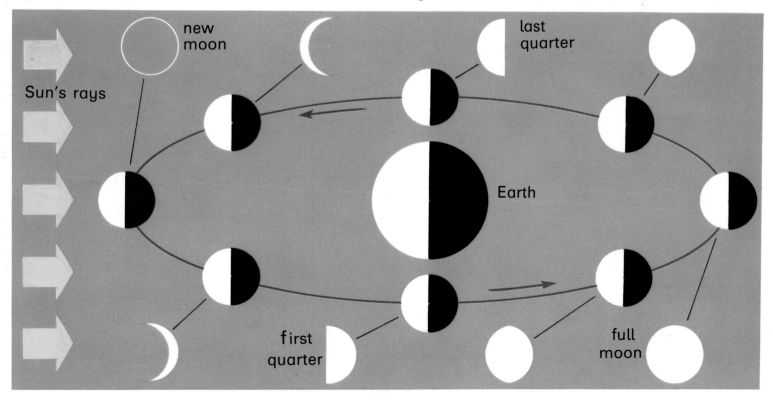

The Sun's family

The Sun is a **giant star**. The Earth is a **planet**. Planets do not give out light of their own. There are nine planets that travel around the Sun, in the same direction (anti-clockwise). Some of the planets are near to the Sun and some are far away.

n Mercury   Venus   Earth   Mars   asteroid belt   Jupiter

The Sun is at the centre. Nearest to the Sun is Mercury. Then comes Venus—Earth—Mars—Jupiter—Saturn—Uranus —Neptune—and Pluto. Jupiter, Saturn, Uranus and Neptune are much bigger than the other planets. They are called **giant planets**.

Uranus   Saturn   Pluto   Neptune

PEOPLE
and the
MAN-MADE WORLD

PEOPLE
On the land

There are millions of people all over the world, and each of us is different. We come in many shapes, sizes and colours. The countries that we live in can be hot, cold, wet or dry. We wear different clothes to suit where we live.

Polynesia

China

India

Russia

Mexico

USA

Iceland

Nigeria

The **shortest woman** is 61 cm (24 inches). The **shortest man** is 67 cm (26½ inches).

The **average height** for a man is 178 cm (5 ft 10 in). The average height for a woman is 165 cm (5 ft 5 in).

The **tallest man** is 272 cm (8 feet 11 inches) and the **tallest woman** is 246 cm (8 feet 1 inch).

pygmies

The **tallest group of people** are the herdsmen of Rwanda and Burundi. They come from Central Africa.

The **shortest group of people** are the Mbuti pygmies. They live in the forests of Zaire in Africa.

Different ideas of beauty

All over the world people decorate themselves. In different countries, the ideas of what is beautiful are not always the same.

Some tribes in Africa decorate their ears. Children have their ears pierced when they are seven. Small discs are forced inside the holes, to stretch them. As the skin stretches, larger discs are used, until the skin is stretched around a huge decorated earring.

Women of the **Padaung tribe** in Burma wear brass rings around their necks. When a Padaung girl is five the first ring is put around her neck. As she gets older, more rings are added. They are very heavy. Some weigh 9 kg (20 lbs).

It is the men of the **Wodaabe tribe** in Africa that make themselves beautiful. They lighten their skins with a special powder and paint their faces. Then the men stand in a circle and the women choose their husbands.

Ways of greeting

There are many countries in the world. People from each country have their own ideas and customs. They have different ideas of what to wear, what looks nice, and what is polite.

In **India** the polite way to greet each other is to join hands, like praying.

In **Russia** people hug each other.

In **Japan** people bow to each other.

In **France** it is the custom to kiss each other on both cheeks.

In **Germany** and many other countries, business men and women shake hands.

In **Alaska** the Innuit (Eskimos) rub noses when they say 'hello'.

Schools

Children all over the world go to school, but schools are not always the same. Many children living in hot countries have lessons outside.

Some Australian children
do not go to a school.
They live far from towns,
in the outback. In the
morning they have lessons
over a two-way radio.
It is called the 'School
of the Air'. In the
afternoon they do homework,
which is posted to their
teacher. They meet the
teacher and the other
children once a year at
a special summer school.

Some boys living in Nepal
go to special schools at
the age of 5, to train as
monks. They get up very
early, at 5 a.m. There is
an hour of prayer and
meditation before lessons
begin.

In **Russia**
some children
as young as
three years
old, go to
special music
schools. They
have lessons
and learn to
play musical
instruments.

Children in Tanzania
(Africa) start school very early in the morning. The village craftsmen – basketmakers, potters, weavers and carpenters – teach the children their skills. The children grow maize and groundnuts in the school garden. They make this into a thick porridge, and eat it for their school dinner.

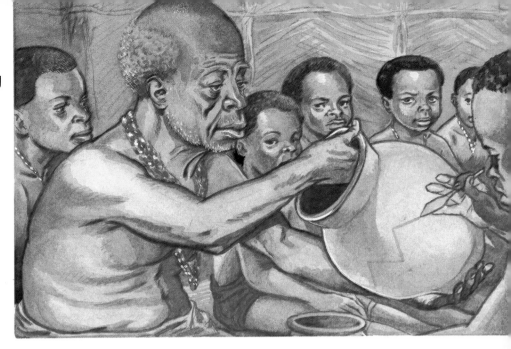

School children in Tokyo
(Japan) play games and sports on the flat roof of the school building. It is such a crowded city that schools do not have playgrounds or playing fields.

Chinese children have exercises every day before lessons. This helps to keep them fit, strong and healthy.

89

Shopping

Many countries in the western world have **hypermarkets**. These are enormous shops, often as big as a football field. All kinds of food, household goods and clothes are sold there. They are usually built outside towns and have large car parks.

In Bangladesh many goods are sold from stalls in **open markets**. It is the custom here, that all the stall holders are men. The women work in the villages.

In Japan most people **shop every day** at local shops and street markets. They like to buy food fresh every day, rather than stock up food for a week or more.

This **market** in Thailand is **on the river**. Some people come in small boats and others come to the water's edge to buy fruit and vegetables.

People who live in the outback of Australia have no shops nearby. Often the shops are so far away that the people have to fly to the towns. They **stock up** and buy enough food to last them several months.

In America and Canada there are **shopping malls**. Many kinds of shops and restaurants are under one roof. Many of the shops have no doors. Whatever the weather outside, it is always dry and warm inside.

Different ways of living

People's lives can be very different. Some countries are rich, some countries are poor.

Los Angeles, in America, is called **'car city'**. Most of the people have cars and they go everywhere in them. They have drive-in banks, movies, shops and even drive-in churches. At drive-in restaurants people sit in their cars to eat.

Many houses in Japan **do not have bathrooms**. Families go to the public bath house to wash. Here there are many large baths with taps around the edge. It is a meeting place. People relax and soak in the water with their friends.

In parts of China, farm workers cannot afford their own television set. Villagers **share one television**. This is watched by as many as 25 families in a large hall.

In Ghana (Africa), villagers **do not have tap water** in their houses. Hundreds of people share one tap. Women bring washing here and carry water back home.

Inside some houses

Bedouin people live in the deserts of Arabia and North Africa. They **live in tents** made with goatskin pieces woven together. The tent has two rooms. The back room is used for cooking and sleeping. The front room is used to entertain visitors.

In the rain forests of Borneo, many families **live together in one long house**. The house is 70 metres (230 feet) wide. There are no inside walls. Each family has its own section, with areas for cooking, washing, eating and sleeping.

In Japan, **houses are very small**. A family of five may have only two small rooms divided by a sliding paper door. They use the same room to live and sleep in. Bedding is rolled up and put away during the day. It is spread out on the floor at night.

Houses

People build houses with the materials that are around them. The kind of house depends upon the weather in that area.

This house is in **Iran** where it is **very hot**. It has no windows. There is only a small opening near the top of the wind tower. Any breeze there is goes down the tower into the house. Thick walls keep it cool inside.

This house is in **Norway** where it is **very cold**. The house is built on a layer of stones to keep it dry. The roof is covered with turf and tree bark. It is very steep so that snow falls off easily.

This house is in **Darwin**, Australia, where it is **very windy**. It was built around a central pillar. When a cyclone (storm) comes, the house sways but it is not blown down.

This house is in **India**, where it is **very wet**. The walls are made of bamboo, covered with thick mud. The roof of rice straw is very steep so that rain runs off quickly.

In **Calcutta** (India) the people are very poor. Their houses are made of cardboard boxes and scraps of metal. They are called **shanty towns**.

Many people in **Singapore** live in **blocks of flats**. These take up less space in this crowded city. They have no gardens, so the people hang washing out of the windows on poles.

On **Madeira Island** (near Africa) the roofs of the houses are thatched and they slope down to the ground.

In **northern Tunisia** (Africa) some people live in **caves**. People who live in caves are called troglodytes. The rooms are cool in the summer and warm in winter.

Police around the world

Every country has a police force. They all wear uniforms to show the job they do.

USA

India

France

Britain

Saudi Arabia

Papua New Guinea

Canada

Working underground

This man is a **coal-face machine driver**. The machine cuts away coal from the coal-face. It weighs 17 tonnes. He cuts out about 150 tonnes of coal every day.

This woman is a **colliery nurse**. She goes down the mine to check the first-aid equipment. Each mine has several First-Aid Stations that have medical equipment to deal with emergencies.

These **gold miners** are carried down into the mine in a steel cage. It travels down through a shaft 1·6 km (1 mile) deep in two minutes. The gold is mined 4 km (2½ miles) below the surface. It is very hot in the gold mines. To keep them cool the men wear special jackets with pockets filled with ice. After a few hours they change their jacket for a new one from the deep freeze.

'A race to the finish'

The **rarajipari**, or **kickball race**, takes place in South America. Two teams of Tarahumara Indians race each other, to kick a wooden ball across mountainous countryside. They wear rattles on their bodies to keep them awake. The race may last several days and cover up to 322 km (200 miles).

The **Iditarod** is the world's longest dog sled race. The course is 1600 km (1000 miles) long, from Anchorage to Nome, in Alaska. Winds of 128 km/h (80 mph), temperatures 45° below zero and snowstorms make this a very difficult race. Only nine of this woman's 15 dogs survived the race. She was suffering from frost-bite as she came to the finish. It had taken her 16 days.

The **Tour de France** is a 25-day cycle race. The riders stop at night and start again in the morning. The course is 4800 km (3000 miles).

Hundreds of people run in the **London Marathon**, but not all finish. The course is 42·2 km (26 miles 385 yds) long. The fastest time is 2 hr 7 m 11 s.

Sports

The world's fastest ball game is **pelota**. It is played in Mexico. The two players have scoops strapped to their arms. The hard elastic ball is caught in the scoop and tossed out. It travels at lightning speed against the walls of the court. The ball can travel at 320 km/h (200 mph).

Sumo wrestling is the oldest sport in Japan. The wrestlers are very fat and heavy. They eat huge meals to put on extra weight. The contest lasts only a few minutes. The winner is the wrestler who throws his opponent to the ground out of the ring.

Soccer is the most popular football sport. It is played in nearly every country in the world. Many countries compete for the famous World Cup. The finals are held every four years.

In the water
Sports

Cave diving is a dangerous sport. The divers explore underground rivers and caves. They have lights on their helmets to help them find their way in the darkness.

Target divers dive from a height of 40 m (130 ft). The tank has a target painted on the bottom and each diver tries to hit the bull's-eye.

Water polo is a team sport played in many countries. Each team has seven players. The players swim, dribble and pass the ball. They can catch or throw the ball using only one hand.

In **ski-kiting** the skier holds a large, light kite. As the skier is towed along at speed, she is lifted into the air. She can glide for several minutes before landing.

In **ski-jumping** a boat is driven in a straight line about 5 m (15 feet) to the right of a jumping ramp. The skier is pulled up the ramp and takes off into the air. Good jumpers can soar many metres through the air and land safely.

Race walking is a sport in Polynesia. A course is marked out on the seabed, using wooden pegs. It is about 63 m (70 yds) long. The walkers carry a heavy stone to keep them under the water. They are not allowed to swim. They must walk the course. The water is very clear and they are watched by people in boats on the surface.

Houses above water

In **Thailand** some people live in **houses built on stilts**. They have flooded their land so that they can grow rice and catch fish.

In **Peru**, people live on Lake Titicaca which is the highest inland sea in the world. By planting totara reeds they have made islands. The reeds grow down 1·8 m (6 ft) into the water. The people build their huts on top of the reeds. The totara reed is used for many things – building huts and making boats, bedmats and baskets.

In **Hong Kong** there is a **floating village** called Aberdeen. There are 4000 boats, shops and temples. Families live on boats called junks. Other boats called sampans are used for fishing.

Houses under water

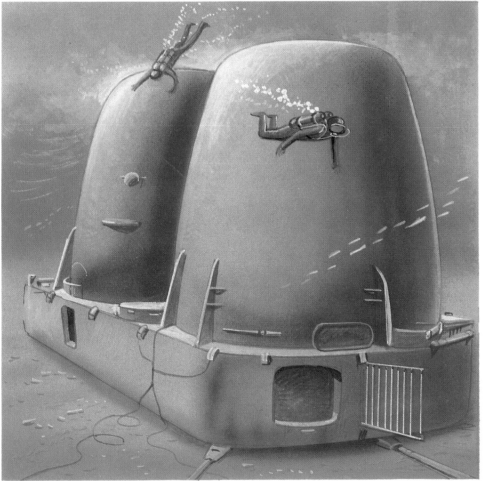

the underwater hatch (door) into Tektite

Tektite is an American experimental craft. It was built to see how long people can live and work under the sea. It was lowered 15 metres (50 feet) into the sea. Crews of divers lived in Tektite for eight weeks.

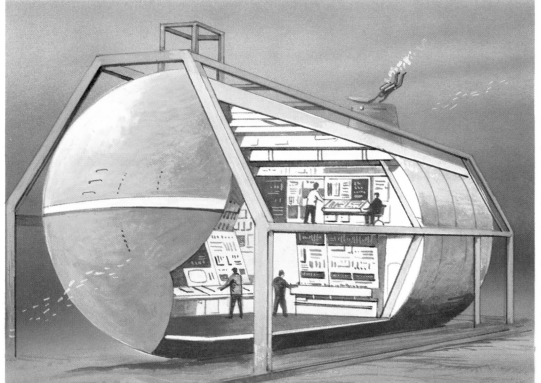

Hydrolab is another American underwater habitat (home). People living under the sea are called **aquanauts**. Hydrolab rests on the seabed. The teams of divers explore and carry out experiments.

Working under the sea

Film companies employ **underwater cameramen and women**. They use special waterproof cameras. This skin diver is filming a coral reef and the animals that live there. She breathes air through tubes from an aqualung strapped on her back. She is working 10 m (30 feet) down. The air in the tank will last for about 40 minutes.

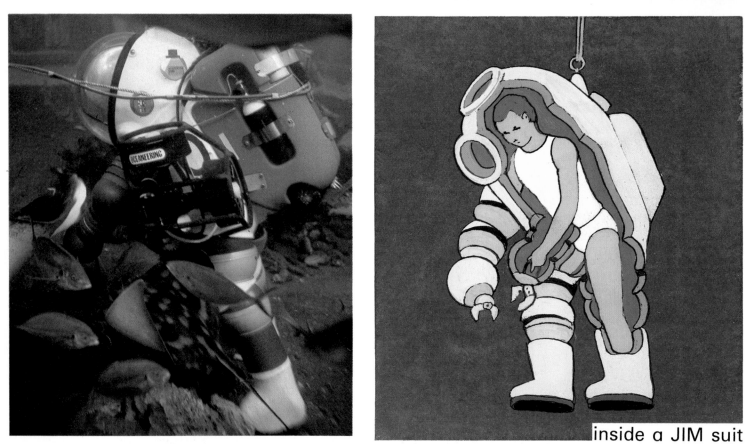

inside a JIM suit

This is a **deep-sea diver**. He is wearing a strong diving suit called a JIM. With this suit on, a deep-sea diver can work 500 m (1640 ft) down and can stay under water for a long time. Out of the water, the suit weighs half a tonne. However, the diver can move about easily under the water. With the special metal hands of the suit, the diver can pick up small objects.

Pearl divers collect oysters from the seabed. They are found about 15–30 m (50–100 ft) below the surface. They do not wear breathing equipment, but can hold their breath for several minutes. They carry sharp knives to cut the oysters away from the coral. It is difficult and dangerous work. There are many sharks in these warm Pacific waters.

One diver is **mending an oil pipeline** under the sea. The other diver is checking the pipe. He uses a scuba scooter to pull himself along through the water.

Unusual ways of fishing

Some **tribes in South America** have a special way of catching fish. They collect poisonous plants, crush them and put them in a basket in the river. The poison is carried downstream in the water. The poison makes the fish sleepy and they swim very slowly. Then it is easy for the men to spear and catch the fish.

These **Japanese fishermen** use birds to help them catch fish. Cormorants are tied to the small boat. They dive down into the water, bringing the fish up in their beaks. Rope is tied round their necks so that they cannot swallow the fish. The men fish at night and the light from lanterns attracts fish to the boat.

Some fishermen in Canada fish from inside a hut, on a frozen lake. The hut has a hole in the floor. A hole is cut through the ice. The fisherman sits and dangles his line through the hole in the floor, into the water.

Emergency services

The Navy and Air Force work closely with the Coastguards to provide a search and rescue service. All the crews wear lifejackets and carry medical equipment. It is a dangerous job as rescues often take place in rough seas and stormy weather.

This boy fell down a cliff. A large lifeboat cannot get near the cliff, so an **inflatable lifeboat** is used. The boy is badly hurt. He is strapped to a stretcher. Then he is winched up into the **RAF rescue helicopter** and taken to hospital.

This ship has sent a distress signal to the Coastguard. She is in danger of sinking. A **lifeboat** and a **Navy Sea King helicopter** have come to the rescue. The helicopter uses its powerful searchlights to light up the sea. Many people clamber aboard the lifeboat. Others are on a life-raft. They are winched up, one by one, into the safety of the helicopter.

In the air
Emergency services

In Australia there is a **flying doctor service**. Many people live on farms which are miles from the nearest town. They call for help, in an emergency, using a two-way radio. The planes have room for one stretcher patient, a sitting patient, the doctor and the pilot. Anyone seriously ill is flown to the nearest hospital.

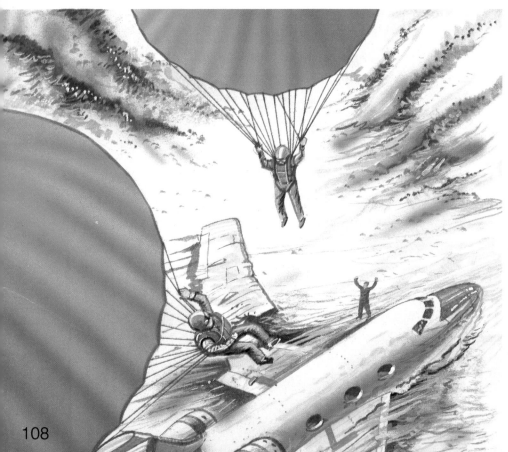

In America they have a new emergency service called **para-rescue**. People are dropped by parachute, to help anyone in trouble. They are trained in many skills because they deal with many different kinds of emergency. They are taught parachuting, first-aid, mountaineering, arctic survival and skin diving.

Space

The **first man in Space** was Yuri Gagarin. He was a Russian Air Force major. In 1961 he orbited the earth in his spacecraft 'Vostok I'.

The **first woman in Space** was Valentina Tereshkova. She travelled in 'Vostok II' in 1963. The Russians call their people in Space **cosmonauts**.

The **first man on the Moon** was Neil Armstrong. He took this photograph of the second man to step on to the Moon, Edwin Aldrin. They landed on the Moon in 1969 and collected samples (pieces) of moon rock. Americans call their people in Space **astronauts**.

The first **free-flight in Space** was made by Captain McCandless and Lieutenant Colonel Stewart in 1984. They were on a mission in the Space Shuttle 'Challenger'. They wore special back packs, which have 24 gas jets to move them around.

Living in Space

The Earth pulls everything towards it. The pull (or force) is called **gravity**. In Space there is no gravity and everything floats. This makes living in Space very different and sometimes difficult.

Sleeping – astronauts have special beds fixed to the walls. They sleep upright, strapped into their sleeping bags.

Eating and drinking – food comes ready made in plastic packs. If it is dry, they squirt water into the bag to mix the food. They squirt drinks into their mouths through a tube.

Exercise – it is important to exercise. Inside the spacecraft they have special pedalling machines.

Washing – astronauts shower inside a special bag that is fixed to the ceiling.

Spacesuits – if astronauts leave the spacecraft, they must wear a special spacesuit. This protects them from the heat of the Sun's rays and the freezing cold of Space. Inside the suit is air for them to breathe and a radio so that they can talk to the others.

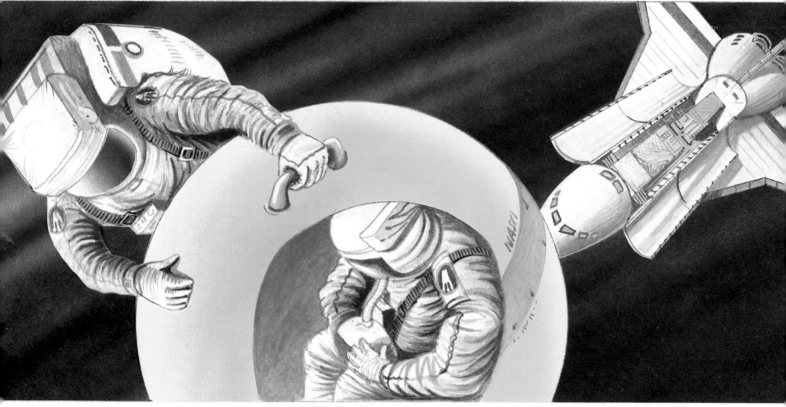

Rescue – if all the astronauts have to leave their spacecraft in an emergency, two of them wear spacesuits. The others are zipped into special rescue balls. These are carried to a rescue ship.

Sports

Every year in early May, people in Thailand and Japan have **kite fights**. They tie razor blades and broken glass on to the edges of kites. The huge kites are flown by a team. They try to cut up the other team's kite. The winners are the team whose kite is left in the air.

Hang gliding is a world-wide sport. The gliders use rising air currents and the wind to keep them up. The person can change direction by moving his or her body from side to side.

Sky-diving – these sky-divers jump from an aircraft flying at around 3000 m (10,000 feet). They fall through the air, making patterns in the sky. They will only open their parachutes when they are about 900 m (3000 feet) from the ground.

Flying displays

Many countries have flying aerobatic display teams. The planes make patterns in the sky and show us the great skill of the pilots. The patterns are called formations.

The British team is called the **Red Arrows**.

different formations

The **Thunderbirds** are the American team.

The **Snowbirds** are the Canadian team.

Strange flights

A man in California, USA, has made a **sun-powered balloon**. Hot-air balloons rise when the air inside is warmer than the air outside. A burner is used to launch the balloon. Then the heat from the Sun takes over. One side of the balloon is black and the other side is clear plastic. Sunlight shines through the plastic side, hits the black side and is trapped inside the balloon. To land, battery-operated propellors turn the clear side away from the Sun and the balloon slowly descends (comes down).

Four men made a **balloon flight across the Pacific Ocean** in 1981. They flew in a balloon called 'Double Eagle V', from Japan to California, USA. They travelled 9282 km (5768 miles) across the Pacific Ocean. It took them four days and five nights. They tried to reach a height of 7925 km (26,000 feet), but it was so cold that ice formed on the balloon and they had to fly lower.

In 1982 this man flew across the English Channel in a flying machine called **Gossamer Albatross**. It weighs 34 kg (75 lbs) and has no engine. The only source of power is its pedals. It took three hours to cover the 33½ km (21 miles) across the Channel.

Setting a goal

On land, in water and in the air, people risk their lives to set new records. Often these adventures are very dangerous.

Two men set out to **climb a frozen waterfall** in Switzerland. It was 152 m (500 ft) high. They used ice axes and shoes with sharp spikes to dig into the ice. Part of the climb was up a curtain of ice which hung clear of the rock. They finished the climb before warmer weather set in and the ice melted.

This **long-distance swimmer** from India achieved four incredible swims in one year. In April he swam the Palk Strait from India to Sri Lanka. In August he swam across the Strait of Gibraltar, from Europe to Africa. In September he swam the Dardanelles, from Europe to Turkey. In October he swam the entire length of the Panama Canal. His name is Mihir Sen.

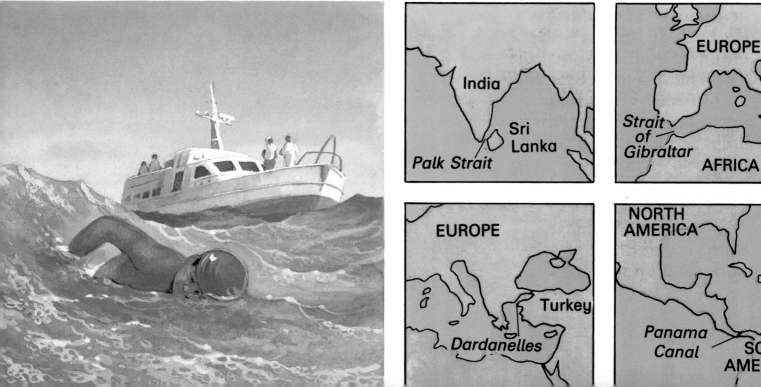

This **hot-air balloon** was called 'Explorer II'. In 1935 this giant balloon went up to a height of 22 km (72,395 feet) above the Earth. It was the highest anyone had ever been. This record lasted for 22 years. Since 1935 many people have ascended (gone up) to greater heights. Now hot-air balloons go up to the edge of Space. When people go this high they wear special pressure suits, like astronauts.

This woman **sailed round the world single-handed** (on her own), in her yacht 'Express Crusader'. Her name is Naomi Lewis. She covered 48,278 km (30,000 miles) in nine months. She travelled 209 km (130 miles) every day.

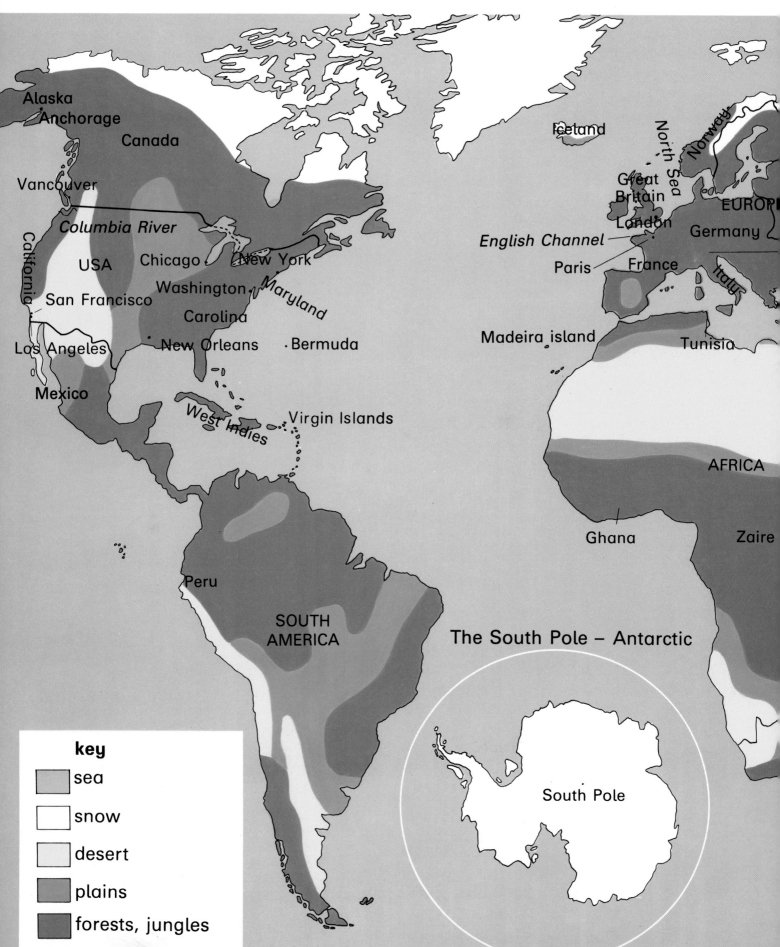

MAP OF

Alaska
Anchorage
Canada
Vancouver
Columbia River
California
USA
Chicago
New York
San Francisco
Washington
Maryland
Carolina
Los Angeles
New Orleans
Bermuda
Mexico
West Indies
Virgin Islands

Peru

SOUTH
AMERICA

Iceland
North Sea
Norway
Great
Britain
London
EUROPE
English Channel
Germany
Paris
France
Italy
Madeira island
Tunisia

AFRICA

Ghana
Zaire

The South Pole – Antarctic

South Pole

key
sea
snow
desert
plains
forests, jungles

THE WORLD

USSR (Russia)

Switzerland

Turkey

Iran

Afghanistan

ASIA

Nepal

Agra

Calcutta

India

Arabia

Sri Lanka

China

Bangladesh

Thailand

Hong Kong

Singapore

Borneo

Japan

Honshú

Tokyo

Shikoku

Pacific Ocean

Polynesia

Darwin

Australia

Sydney

New Zealand

anzania

The North Pole – Arctic

Arctic Ocean

North Pole

MAN-MADE WORLD
On the land

IT'S A RECORD

The St Gotthard **road tunnel** in Switzerland is the longest road tunnel in the world. It is 16·32 km (10·14 miles) long. It has two lanes of traffic and it runs from Göschenen to Airolo.

Tokyo is the biggest city in the world. It is in Japan. There are 11 million people living and working there.

'Thrust 2' is the fastest jet engine on wheels. This car achieved the land speed record, in the Nevada desert, USA, in 1984. It travelled at a speed of 1035 km/h (643 mph). It is the fastest British car.

The United States of America is the **country with the most roads**. They have more than 6,000,000 km (3,728,400 miles) of roadway. The fastest roads are called freeways. In different countries, fast roads have different names: in France – autoroute; Germany – autobahn; Italy – autostrada; England – motorway. The Los Angeles Freeway carries traffic quickly through the city.

Venice, in Italy, is the only city in the world that has no roads. It has only footpaths and canals.

The **Sears Tower** in Chicago, USA, is the tallest office building in the world. It is 443 m (1454 feet) high. There are 110 floors (storeys) with 16,700 people working there. It has 103 elevators, 18 escalators and 16,000 windows.

How we use computers

Computers are a great help to us. They can work very fast and do many jobs at once. They have made new inventions possible.

Microcomputers are the smallest computers. Scientists found they could print electronic circuits on to a single, tiny chip of silicon. These **microprocessors** work faster. Some silicon chips are used for memory, to store information. Microprocessors are found in pocket calculators, digital watches and desk-top computers. They also control many machines and electronic toys. We can program the cooker to switch itself on and off.

a single silicon chip

digital watch

automatic cooker

electronic toy

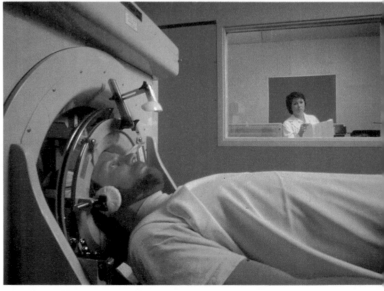

Newspaper and magazine printers use computers to arrange the text (writing) and the pictures on a page, ready for printing.

Hospitals use computers. X-ray scanners take many pictures. The computer sorts them and shows them on a television screen.

The **Police** use computers to control traffic lights in busy cities. In the central control room, the Police can watch out for traffic jams.

This **car factory** uses robots which are controlled by computers. The robots do paint spraying and welding jobs. They can work very quickly. They can weld (join) the metal in 250 places in 23 seconds.

The **underground railway** in San Francisco (USA) is controlled by a computer system. It is called BART (the Bay Area Rapid Transit system). There is no driver.

Flight simulators are used to train airline pilots. Inside the simulator it feels as if you are flying in an aircraft. The huge machine is on legs. A computer makes the legs move. Instead of windows there are television screens. The computer can show pictures on these of all the main airports around the world, day or night. This means pilots can practise landing an aircraft.

Trains

The **fastest train** in the world is the French TGV. It travels between Paris and Lyon at 298 km/h (185 mph). It is so fast that it needs 3·2 km (2 miles) to slow down and stop.

In Wuppertal in West Germany there is a **monorail**. This is a train that hangs down from an overhead rail. The track is 20 m (65½ feet) above the ground.

In Birmingham, England, there is a new **magnetic train**, called Mag-Lev. There are four pairs of magnets on each side of the train which lift it 15 mm (⅗ inch) above the track.

The Metro train at Lille, France, is an **underground train**. It is controlled by computer. There is no driver or guard. Passengers get their tickets from machines.

Cable railways have
no engines. They are
pulled up and down steep
slopes by cables. There are
two tracks, side by side.
As one train comes down, the
other one is pulled up.

Mountain railways are called rack
and pinion railways. They run on
a special track. A third rail in the
middle of the track has teeth on
it. A wheel under the train also
has teeth. This is the **pinion**. The
teeth fit into the **rack** on the track.
This stops the train slipping backwards.

The railway up Mount Pilatus in
Switzerland is the steepest **rack
and pinion** railway in the world.
Inside the cars, the seats go up
in steps. This stops the people
from falling out of their seats
as the train goes up the steep
mountainside.

Monster machines

This **house-mover** is a **lift rig** weighing 200 tonnes. It picks up houses that are to be moved and takes them to a new place.

The **Arctic Snow Train** has 54 wheels and is the longest vehicle ever built. It is 174·3 m (572 feet) long and has a top speed of 32 km/h (20 mph).

This is the **longest bus in the world**. It works in the Middle East oil-fields, carrying people to work. It is 23 m (76 feet) long. It can carry 187 passengers (121 sitting and 66 standing).

This **transporter** (right) was built to carry space rockets. It is 39·9 m (131 ft) long, 35 m (114 ft) wide and 6 m (20 ft) high. It moves at a speed of 1·6 km/h (1 mph).

This **mining dump truck** can carry 77,000 kg (76 tons) of rock and earth. Its engine is as powerful as 11 cars. It has seven forward and one reverse (backward) gears.

Big Muskie is a dragline excavator. It works in open cast mines. A small house would fit inside its huge bucket, which holds 200,000 kg (1968 tonnes).

Famous buildings – old and new

The **Taj Mahal** at Agra in India took 20 years to build. Its white marble walls have been carved by hand and inlaid with patterns using semi-precious stones. Shah Jahan ordered it to be built as a memory to his young wife when she died. It is surrounded by gardens.

The **Great Pyramid** at Giza in Egypt was built over 4500 years ago. One hundred thousand slaves moved and lifted more than two million stone slabs to build the pyramid. It took 30 years to complete. Inside there are chambers where the Pharaohs and Queens were buried.

The **Great Wall of China** was built in the third century BC (Before Christ). It is 6325 km (3930 miles) long, 12 m (39 feet) high and 10 m (32 feet) thick. The Great Wall is the only man-made structure that can be seen from Space.

The **Leaning Tower of Pisa**, in Italy, has eight storeys. When the builders reached the third storey it began to lean over. This may be because it was built on sand. They finished building it, but each year it leans over more. One day it may fall down.

The **Pompidou Centre** is in Paris.
All the walls are made of glass, built
on a steel frame. A moving staircase
goes all the way up the building, on
the outside. Inside there are art
galleries, a library and a cinema.

The **Sydney Opera House** is in
Australia. It is built on land
jutting out into Sydney Harbour.
The roof is made of 10 shells.
The highest shell is 75 metres
(221 feet) above the water.

The tallest tower is in
Toronto, Canada. It is the
Canadian National Tower.
It is 555 metres (1821
feet) tall.

129

Statues

The tallest statue in the world is in Russia. It is called **'Motherland'**. It is 82 m (270 feet) high.

The **Statue of Liberty** stands on Liberty island, at the entrance to New York harbour.

The **Great Buddha** is in Afghanistan. It was built by monks 1500 years ago.

The **Mount Rushmore Sculptures** in America are four giant heads each 18 m (60 ft) high. They are carved out of the rock. The faces are of four American presidents – George Washington, Thomas Jefferson, Theodore Roosevelt and Abraham Lincoln.

On **Easter Island**, in the Pacific Ocean, there are nearly 1000 statues. They are huge carved heads. It is believed that they are of their past chiefs. Three hundred of them are on platforms around the coast. All of these face inland.

Bridges

Sydney Harbour bridge is the widest long-span bridge in the world. It has two electric railway tracks, eight lanes of roadway, one cycle track and one footpath.

The **Lake Pontchartrain Causeway** is the longest bridge. It is near New Orleans in America. It is 38½ km (nearly 24 miles) long. It is so long that when you are in the middle you cannot see the land on either side.

The **Humber Bridge** in England has the longest gap between its main supports. The distance between the two towers is 1410m (4626 ft). Each tower rises to a height of 162m (530 ft). As the Earth's surface is curved, the towers are farther apart at the top than at the bottom.

Power and energy

Electricity is an important source of power and energy. It is made in many different ways. We can use water, the wind and the sun to make electricity.

The **Grand Coulee Dam** on the Columbia River, in Washington, USA, is the largest concrete dam in the world. It is 1272 m (4173 feet) long and 167 m (548 feet) high.

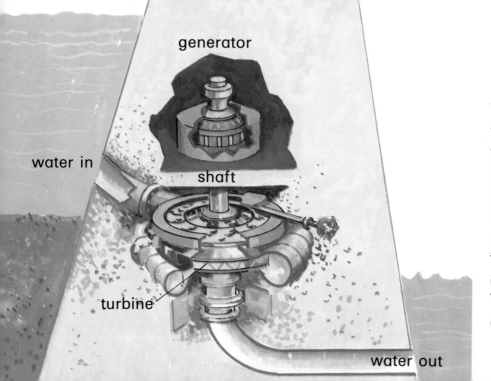

generator

water in

shaft

turbine

water out

To make **electricity**, water from behind the dam rushes through pipes at the bottom. It moves so fast along the pipes that it makes a big wheel (turbine) spin. The turbine drives a machine called a generator. The generator makes electricity.

Many countries in the world are seeking other sources of power. This could be a wind machine of the future. It turns offshore winds into electricity. Each propeller is 18m (60 feet) long.

This **solar (sun) power station** at Odeillo makes electricity that is used all over France. The huge mirrors reflect sunlight on to a furnace. The temperature in the furnace reaches nearly 4000°C.

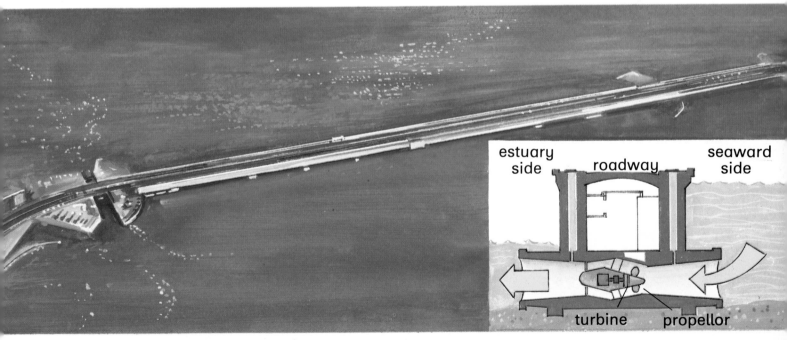

The **Rance Barrage** is a **tidal power station** in France. A huge wall (barrage) has been built across the mouth of the river. The tide rises and falls 13 m (42½ feet) every day. The water is used to drive underwater turbines to make electricity.

In the water

Oil rigs

Oil is very important to us. Sometimes it is called 'liquid gold'. No machine can work without oil. Oil is fuel for cars and trucks, aircraft and ships. It is used in factories and power stations, and for heating. Oil can be found under deserts, under snow and ice, and under the sea. Oil collects in pools, deep down under the earth. These are called wells.

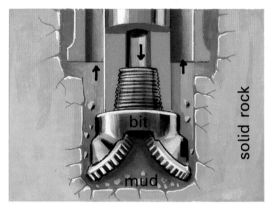

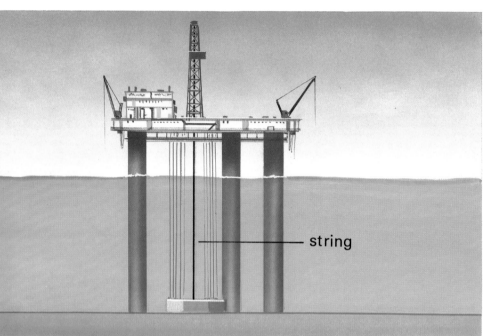

In the North Sea, **drilling rigs** work in water up to 300 m (1000 feet) deep. The oil can be another 3000 m (10,000 feet) under the seabed.

The drilling rig uses a drill to cut through the rock. The drill has a sharp tip at the end called a **bit**. The bit is studded with diamonds, which are the hardest stones.

The rest of the drill is called the **string**, which is a lot of metal pipes joined together. As the drill goes deeper, more pipes are added.

In very deep water, 6 km (3½ miles), a **drill ship** is used. The drilling bit and the drill string go down into the water, through a hole in the bottom of the ship.

A **support ship** guards the drill ship in the Arctic Ocean. Huge floating icebergs might crash into the drill ship. When an iceberg gets too near, a tow rope is fixed around the iceberg. Then it is towed out of the way. This ship can tow icebergs weighing up to 100 million tonnes.

When the drilling rigs have found oil a **production platform** is fixed into place. The drilling pipes pass down, inside the legs of the platform. As many as 40 wells can be drilled from one platform.

The oil now needs to be brought ashore. Sometimes it is piped to an **oil tanker** at sea, or it is carried in pipes under the sea to the shore.

Underwater craft

Submersibles are underwater craft. They are smaller than submarines and are carried on a ship. They are lowered into the sea. Special arms, cameras and equipment are fixed on to the outside.

'**NEMO**' has clear plastic walls. Two people can sit inside and watch underwater building and repair work. 'NEMO' has special electric plugs fitted on the outside, so that divers can use lights and power tools.

OBSS (Ocean Bottom Scanning Sonar vehicle) is another search vessel. It is pulled along the seabed by a cable attached to a ship on the surface. Robot machines are used when conditions are too dangerous for people. It is operated by remote control, from the ship above.

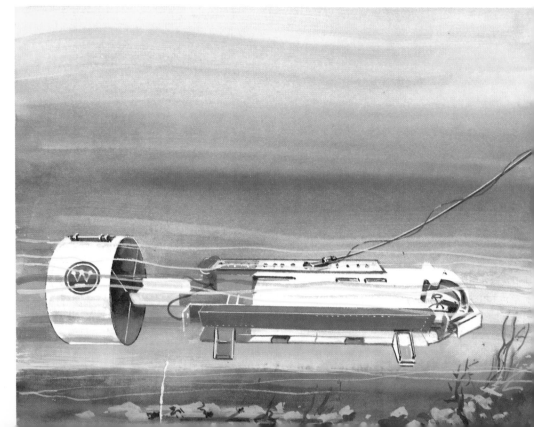

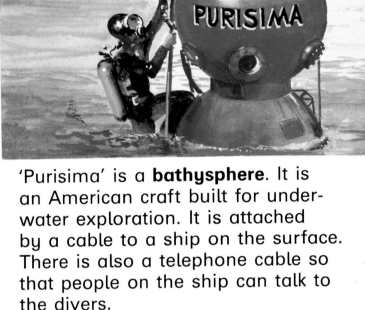

The 'Sea Cat' is used to bury telephone cables under the seabed. The cables are laid by cable ship, but they could be damaged if they rest on the bottom of the sea. The 'Sea Cat' buries them under the sand using special tools.

'Purisima' is a **bathysphere**. It is an American craft built for underwater exploration. It is attached by a cable to a ship on the surface. There is also a telephone cable so that people on the ship can talk to the divers.

Bathyscaphe means 'deep boat'. The 'Trieste' has dived deeper than any other craft, 11·3 km (7 miles). The crew sit in the globe, underneath the ship. They shine powerful lights through the water. Then they film through the windows. The tanks above are filled with petrol and lead balls. These lead balls help the craft to go down. They are unloaded into the sea when the ship comes back up.

Special ships

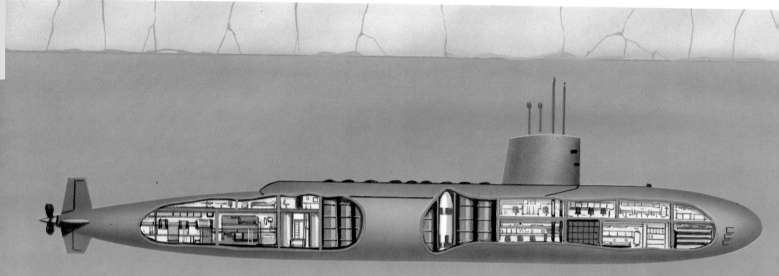

Submarines are big ships that travel under water. They are built with two hulls (bodies), one inside the other. Between the two hulls are ballast tanks. When these tanks are full of air, the submarine floats. When water is let into the tanks, the submarine gets heavier and sinks under water. The 'Nautilus', a nuclear submarine, was the first to travel under the ice at the North Pole.

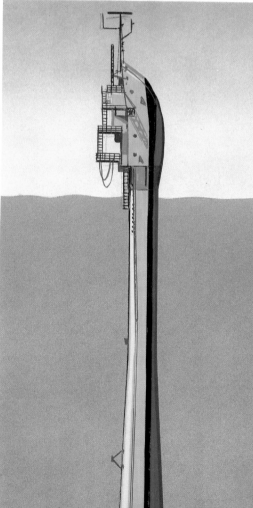

'Flip' is a floating instrument platform. It is a very long ship – 108 m (355 feet) – with no engines. It is towed out to sea. When it is in the right position, it is flooded so that one end sinks and the other end rises up out of the water. Scientists can walk down into the waterproof sections to study the sea and measure the waves.

The 'Shin Aitoku Maru' is a Japanese **sail-assisted tanker**. It has engines like most tankers, but it also has two sets of sails which increase its speed. The sails are 12 m (39 feet) high and 8 m (26 feet) wide.

A **pontoon** is a flat-bottomed boat, used for support. When a bridge has to be built in a hurry, it can be supported by a row of pontoons fixed to the riverbed. Armies use this method, because it is portable.

Sea lanes (routes) are sometimes blocked in bad weather by snow and ice. **Icebreakers** are strengthened ships used to break a path through the ice. The 'Manhattan', the largest icebreaker, is a converted supertanker.

Fire boats are used to put out fires in buildings near seas or on rivers. They have powerful engines to pump up the water to the hoses.

Rescue craft

The **Tyne class lifeboat** is used to save lives around the British coast. It is made of steel and aluminium and is 14·3 m (47 ft) long. It has a top speed of 18 knots. This boat cannot sink. If it is turned over by huge waves, it will come back upright within five seconds.

This **jetboat** is used in Bermuda for rescue work close to the shore, in shallow water and over coral reefs. There are no propellors which could get caught on the rocks and reefs. Its powerful diesel engines suck in sea water and force it out through jets. This pushes the boat forwards.

A **rescue hovercraft** is used by the Canadian Coast Guard. It is based at Vancouver airport. It can skim over floating logs and ice. In good weather it has a speed of 55–60 knots. It is the only hovercraft that is used for rescue work.

The 'John T Essberger' is a large German **rescue cruiser**. There is a small lifeboat, under a helicopter pad, at the stern (back) of the ship. It is 44·5 m (146 feet) long and has three powerful engines. It has a range of 966 km (600 miles) travelling at a speed of 30 knots.

A **rescue submarine** called 'DSRV' is used by the United States Navy. They provide a world-wide rescue service. The 'DSRV' can be carried in an aircraft to anywhere in the world within 24 hours of a disaster. The 'DSRV' is 15 m (49 feet) long and weighs 30 tonnes. It is designed to rescue crews from underwater craft, especially submarines. The bell-shaped skirt under the 'DSRV' fits over the escape hatch on the submarine. It can carry up to 24 people and go back many times, until everyone is safe.

Giants on the sea

The 'USS Enterprise' is the world's largest warship. It is 336 m (1102 feet) long. It is a nuclear-powered ship and can travel very fast – 35 knots. This **aircraft carrier** is a floating base for up to 100 aircraft. There are 4600 members in the crew.

The 'Queen Elizabeth the Second (QE2)' is a huge ocean liner, 293 m (962 feet) long. It is a luxury floating hotel which carries passengers on round-the-world cruises. It has 10 lifeboats on each side of the ship, a theatre, a cinema, a library and a swimming pool.

Water skimmers

This **hovercraft** does not have to push through the water. It hovers just above the surface. This makes it much faster, with a top speed of 65 knots. It skims over the water on a cushion of air. The air, made by powerful fans, is trapped under the craft by a skirt. The hovercraft can also travel on land, over soft mud, marsh and snow. The 'BHC Super 4' is the world's biggest hovercraft. It carries 416 passengers and 55 cars. Each of its four propellors is as high as a house.

A **hydrofoil** also skims above the water. When moving slowly, it travels through the water like a boat. As it gathers speed, it rises up on hydrofoils (underwater wings). This allows it to go faster than ordinary boats. It has a top speed of 80 knots. Because the hull (body) of the boat is above the water, it gives a smooth ride.

In the air

the cockpit of Concorde

Concorde is the fastest passenger airliner. It is powered by
four Rolls Royce turbo jet engines that boost it to speeds of
more than 2300 km/h (1450 mph). It has a needle-shaped nose and
de Ha (triangular) shaped wings. The nose is lowered on take-off
and landing, to give the pilot a better view of the runway.

The '**Super Guppy**' (**C-5A Galaxy**) is
the world's largest aircraft. It was
built to carry parts of space rockets
and has a wing span of 43 m (141 ft).
When it is loaded, a huge door in the
nose swings open.

The **Boeing 747 'Jumbo Jet'**
is the biggest airliner.
It can carry 550 passengers
and 17 crew. The main cabin
is 60 m (197 feet) long and
nearly 7 m (22 feet) wide.

Working aircraft

This is a **rainmaker aircraft**.
In countries where there is little
rain, or a long drought, these planes
are used to make it rain. They fly
above the clouds and drop chemicals
into the clouds. This releases the
water in the clouds – and it rains.

The **'Canadian CL215' amphibious
flying boat** has huge water tanks.
They can hold 5455 litres (1200
gallons) of water. The tanks can be
reloaded by the plane skimming
across the surface of a lake.
It takes only 20 seconds to refill
the tanks with water. The planes
drop the water on forest fires.

On huge ranches in South America
cattle may be scattered over many
miles. **Light aircraft** like this one
are used to track the herds at
round-up time.

In the north of Canada, there are
great areas of forest and many lakes.
Sea planes fly in supplies to people
living in remote places. They have
special floats instead of wheels.

Special aircraft

The **Harrier Jump Jet** can hover, fly sideways and backwards. Unlike ordinary planes, this jet does not need a runway. It can take off, and land, vertically. The jet engines swivel and the force lifts the jet straight up into the air. It can fly at more than 1000 km/h (621 mph).

The **Lockheed Hercules** can fly on long-range journeys. Its vast tanks carry an enormous amount of fuel. This plane is often used to re-fuel smaller aircraft in mid-air. It can carry heavy loads of machinery or troops.

This is a **Japanese amphibian plane**. It is able to land on a runway or on water. The plane can take off, and land, in very rough seas. It is often used to rescue people in danger at sea.

The **Grumman X-29A** is an American experimental plane. It has a new design with forward-sweeping wings. This plane is 15 m (48 ft) long. It can take off and land at lower speeds, on shorter runways, than other fighter aircraft.

The **American F 111** is a swing-wing aircraft. During take-off and landing the wings are fully opened out. As the plane increases speed in the air, the wings fold inwards. Now the plane can fly supersonic (faster than the speed of sound).

Helicopters

Helicopters do not need a runway, unlike most aircraft. They take off, and land, vertically. The engines turn the larger rotor blades (spinning wings) on top and this lifts the helicopter into the air. The smaller rotor blade on the tail is used for steering. They can hover, fly sideways and fly backwards.

This **Russian M1-2 helicopter** is used by the forest protection patrol. It can land anywhere, in a very small space. This helicopter is bringing in extra equipment to fight the fire.

The **autogyro** is different from a helicopter. The engine moves it forwards along the runway and the moving air spins the rotor blade. It cannot hover (stay still) in the air.

The **Sikorsky Sky Crane** is a huge American helicopter used for heavy lifting jobs. It can lift damaged aircraft or huge containers. The Sky Crane can carry 10 tonnes of cargo.

The **Apache** is the United States' newest helicopter. It is used by the Army as an advanced attack helicopter. The Apache has special armoured protection and laser-guided weapons.

Telescopes and satellites

A **telescope** helps us to see far into Space. Inside it there are pieces of glass (lenses) and mirrors. These make stars and planets look bigger, and nearer, than they really are. The telescope can be moved to watch different parts of the sky. The pictures are shown on a screen.

This is a **communications satellite**. It can bounce radio and television signals from one side of the world to the other. Someone in Australia can watch what is happening on American television.

Earth seen from Space

This is a **weather satellite**. It orbits the Earth taking photographs, day and night, using special cameras. It can see how the clouds and winds move. The satellite can warn us of approaching storms.

Machines in Space

The **Space Shuttle** is the first re-usable space-craft. It is launched like a rocket, and flies back to Earth, to land like a plane. It is 37 m (121 feet) from nose to tail. It has delta wings, with a span of 24 m (79 feet). It has five computers on board.

When it is launched, two solid booster rockets and a huge fuel tank are bolted on to it.

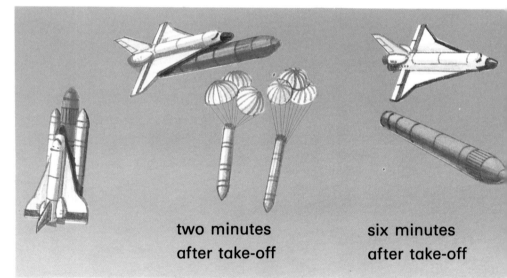

two minutes after take-off

six minutes after take-off

After two minutes' flight, the two solid booster rockets fall away. Six minutes later, at the edge of Space, the empty fuel tank falls away and burns up. The Shuttle's own three rocket engines carry it into Space, where it can stay for up to 30 days.

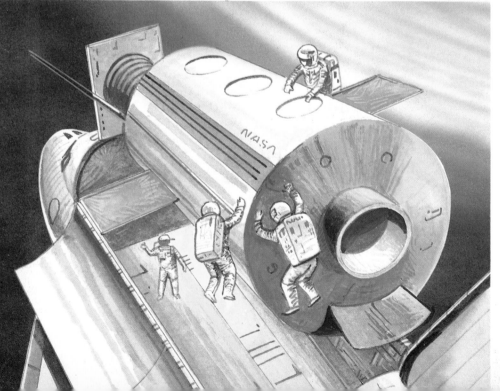

The Shuttle is used to launch new satellites and to repair broken ones. In the future it will carry **Spacelab** into orbit. Spacelab is being built by America, Canada, Japan and 11 European countries. It is a laboratory that fits into the Shuttle's cargo bay, where scientists will carry out experiments.

This special car was used by Amerian astronauts on the Moon. It is called **Lunar Rover Vehicle (LRV)** and is powered by electricity. There are two cameras on it.

The Russian moon car was called **Lunokhod 1**. It roamed over the Moon's surface for nearly a year, sending back photographs of the Moon. It was controlled by a radio on Earth.

Robot explorers

Mariner 9 was the first space probe to give us information about Mars. It sent back television pictures showing giant volcanoes on Mars.

The **Pioneer 10** space probe flew past Jupiter, taking many photographs. It took nearly two years to get there from Earth.

In the making

In Japan they are building a **double deck road–rail bridge**. It will link Honshú and Shikoku. The main span of the bridge will be 1780 m (5840 feet). It will also have side spans, which will make the whole bridge 3560 m (11,680 feet) long. It will be the longest bridge in the world.

The Russians are building a huge earth-filled dam, across the Vakhsh River. It will be called the **Rogunsky dam**. It will be the highest in the world, at 325 m (1066 feet) high. This is an artist's painting.

The United States is building a huge space telescope. It will be 13 m (42½ ft) long and will weigh 10·9 tonnes. The **NASA Space telescope** will see farther out into Space than any telescope on Earth. It will be launched by the Space Shuttle.

The Space Shuttle will launch a new **space probe** called 'Galileo'. The Shuttle will carry it into orbit and it will be boosted on its journey by a rocket. It will travel through space to explore the giant planet Jupiter.

Index